Cambridge Elements

Elements in Women Theatre Makers
edited by
Elaine Aston
Lancaster University
Melissa Sihra
Trinity College Dublin

CARYL CHURCHILL'S ECO-SOCIALIST FEMINISM

Elaine Aston
Lancaster University

Shaftesbury Road, Cambridge CB2 8EA, United Kingdom

One Liberty Plaza, 20th Floor, New York, NY 10006, USA

477 Williamstown Road, Port Melbourne, VIC 3207, Australia

314–321, 3rd Floor, Plot 3, Splendor Forum, Jasola District Centre, New Delhi – 110025, India

103 Penang Road, #05–06/07, Visioncrest Commercial, Singapore 238467

Cambridge University Press is part of Cambridge University Press & Assessment, a department of the University of Cambridge.

We share the University's mission to contribute to society through the pursuit of education, learning and research at the highest international levels of excellence.

www.cambridge.org
Information on this title: www.cambridge.org/9781009534246

DOI: 10.1017/9781009534253

© Elaine Aston 2025

This publication is in copyright. Subject to statutory exception and to the provisions of relevant collective licensing agreements, no reproduction of any part may take place without the written permission of Cambridge University Press & Assessment.

When citing this work, please include a reference to the DOI 10.1017/9781009534253

First published 2025

A catalogue record for this publication is available from the British Library

ISBN 978-1-009-53424-6 Hardback
ISBN 978-1-009-53423-9 Paperback
ISSN 2634-2391 (online)
ISSN 2634-2383 (print)

Cambridge University Press & Assessment has no responsibility for the persistence or accuracy of URLs for external or third-party internet websites referred to in this publication and does not guarantee that any content on such websites is, or will remain, accurate or appropriate.

For EU product safety concerns, contact us at Calle de José Abascal, 56, 1°, 28003 Madrid, Spain, or email eugpsr@cambridge.org

Caryl Churchill's Eco-Socialist Feminism

Elements in Women Theatre Makers

DOI: 10.1017/9781009534253
First published online: October 2025

Elaine Aston
Lancaster University
Author for correspondence: Elaine Aston, e.aston@lancaster.ac.uk

Abstract: Pivotal to Caryl Churchill's *What If If Only* (2021) is the ghost of a democratic future that never happened. Framed by *What If If Only*, if-only yearnings for a democratic future are seminal to this Element with its primary attention to the feminist, socialist, and ecological values of Churchill's theatre. Arguing for the triangulation of the latter, the study elicits insights into: the feeling structures of Churchill's plays; reparative strategies for the renewal of an eco-feminist-socialist politics; the conceptualisation of the 'political is personal' to understand the negative emotional impact that an anti-egalitarian regime has on people's lives; and relations between dystopian criticality and utopian desire. Hannah Proctor's notion of 'anti-adaptive healing' is invoked to propose a summative understanding of Churchill's theatre as engaging audiences in anti-adaptive, resistant feelings towards a capitalist order and healing through a utopic sensing that an alternative future is desirable and still possible.

Keywords: Caryl Churchill, feminism, socialism, ecology, theatre

© Elaine Aston 2025
ISBNs: 9781009534246 (HB), 9781009534239 (PB), 9781009534253 (OC)
ISSNs: 2634-2391 (online), 2634-2383 (print)

Contents

Introduction	1
1 Structures of Feminist Feeling	3
2 Against 'The Great Moving Right Show'	17
3 The Political is Personal	33
4 Towards a Theatre of 'Anti-Adaptive Healing'	48
References	61

Introduction

In the autumn of 2021, at the Royal Court Theatre, London, the stage was set for Caryl Churchill's elliptical, poetic, short play, *What If If Only*.[1] 'Someone', played by John Heffernan, sits at a table facing an empty chair, vacant because his loved one, his partner, has died – seemingly committed suicide. Could they not make contact, come back, talk to him, he laments. As his grief intensifies, the revenant who joins him is not his partner but 'the ghost of a future that never happened' (Churchill 2021: 9). This spirited and at times darkly funny manifestation performed by Linda Bassett expounds on the future that might have been: 'Equality and cake and no bad bits at all' (Churchill 2021: 10). Thus, a tableau of private, personal grief shapeshifts into a political voicing of a democratic future lost to a dystopian present.

Haunted by the spectre of the Covid-19 pandemic, Churchill's uncanny reckoning touched a contemporary nerve given the worldwide grieving for the millions of lives lost to the virus, and questions about post-pandemic futures. But coming at this advanced stage of Churchill's career that now spans over sixty years, *What If If Only* is also infused with a retrospective feeling: a spirited lamentation for an alternative future that has haunted Churchillian landscapes, past and present. Time and again, Churchill has returned to the notion of socially progressive and ecologically sustainable futures damaged or destroyed by systems of capitalist and patriarchal power. And yet, as *What If If Only* exemplifies, the future that might have been is not laid to rest but returns, calling on Someone 'to make me real' (Churchill 2021: 10).

Inspired and framed by *What If If Only*, this Element is also a kind of revenant: a revisitation of Churchill's playwriting that has haunted the years of my own interests in the vicissitudes of feminist theatre. Its scope is not wide-ranging: this is not an attempt to distil the entirety of Churchill's oeuvre into a general overview. Rather, the Element focuses on the feminist, socialist and ecological dimensions and dynamics of Churchill's political theatre. Ultimately, I posit their triangulation as the basis on which Churchill demonstrates a socially progressive and ecologically sustainable future as politically desirable, critically urgent, and still possible.

The first three sections form a chronological triptych: Churchill in the revolutionary years of 1970s, second-wave feminism; her opposition to the rise of the Right in the 1980s and the long shadow cast by Thatcherite ideology; her millennial and twenty-first-century turn to the disconnect between the personal and the political, and the dystopic reckonings of a unipolar world enmeshed in the forces of Western capitalism. Each of these sections draws on

---

[1] *What If If Only* opened on 29 September 2021 in the Royal Court's Theatre Downstairs.

a trio of plays: Section 1, *Owners* (1972), *Vinegar Tom* (1976), and *Light Shining in Buckinghamshire* (1976); Section 2, *Top Girls* (1982), *Fen* (1983), *The Skriker* (1994); and Section 3, *This Is a Chair* (1997), *Far Away* (2000), *Escaped Alone* (2016). These are by no means the only plays I might have chosen, but I made my selection on the basis that each of them affords a seminal insight into or reflection on facets of Churchill's eco-socialist-feminist politics.

As this chronological triptych traces the shapeshifting formations of Churchill's political theatre-making over the decades, the economic, social and ecological outlook appears increasingly dystopian. *What If If Only*'s spirit complains that the 'enemies' of a 'better' future deny there is an alternative to the dystopian present – dismissing such a possibility as 'a utopia nowhere place' (Churchill 2021: 10). And yet a Churchillian dystopic is shadowed by a utopic sensing that things can be otherwise. Hence, to elucidate how dystopian criticality is twinned with the utopic impulse to desire and live differently, the concluding, fourth section circles back to the 1970s – to the dystopian mode of Churchill's radio play, *Not Not Not Not Not Enough Oxygen* (1971) and utopian-themed *Cloud Nine* (1979). In turn, this focus on dystopian critique and desiring differently paves the way for a summative understanding of Churchill's theatre as a site of 'anti-adaptive healing' (Proctor 2024) – as potentially engaging spectators in anti-adaptive, resistant feelings towards a capitalist order, and healing through a utopian sensing that an alternative future is desirable and still possible.

Methodologically, because this Element primarily engages in a revisitation of plays by Churchill, rather than analysis of new works undertaken in or close to their moment of production, the dramatic text figures largely in discussion, albeit variously punctuated with details of original stagings, archival traces and personal recollections of performances. The critical-theoretical literature that accompanies analysis of the plays is chiefly, though not strictly, contemporaneous with the time of their production. This includes, but is not limited to: Raymond Williams' 'structures of feeling' (1977); Juliet Mitchell on feminism and 'speaking bitterness' (1971); Stuart Hall's analysis of socialism's 'hard road to renewal' (1988); Beatrix Campbell on Margaret Thatcher's 'iron ladies' (1987); the ecofeminist insights of Françoise d'Eaubonne (2022 [1974]) and Val Plumwood (1993); Troy Vettese and Drew Pendergrass' proposal for a 'half-earth socialism' (2022); and Hannah Proctor on the psychological toll of surviving in and beyond political struggles (2024). These critical and political touchstones assist my analysis and cumulative understanding of Churchill's triangulated attentions to feminism, socialism, and ecology.

Although the 'enemies' of a democratic future have escalated over the years, turning now to the 1970s, I revisit the decade in which second-wave feminism befriended a future enshrined in 'Equality and cake and no bad bits at all' (Churchill 2021: 10).

1 Structures of Feminist Feeling

To return to the 1970s is to revisit a decade haunted by the feminist future that might have been. A vibrant women's movement gathered momentum and protested inequalities and social injustices on a scale not seen since the years of women's suffrage at the turn of the twentieth century. This feminist awakening, or rather re-awakening, was ignited by women's widespread, everyday experiences of inequality. The experiential basis of their discontents elicited a political awareness: as women shared and debated their experiences in and among a burgeoning number of organically formed groups, they engaged in a mode of consciousness-raising that connected the personal to the political. Hence, the second-wave feminist mantra, 'the personal is political'.

This experiential mode of coming-to-feminist-consciousness resonates with Raymond Williams' 'structures of feeling' as 'concerned with meanings and values as they are actively lived and felt' (1977: 132): a way to recognise the 'practical consciousness' of 'what is actually being lived, and not only what it is thought is being lived' (1977: 130–131). By this account, women's 'practical consciousness' of oppression is what gives rise to renewed structures of feminist feeling. It is the experience of living and *feeling* structures of oppression that fosters affectively realised attachments to feminism.

As Williams further observed, it is the arts that allow us to access a 'felt sense of the quality of life at a particular place and time' that is otherwise difficult to grasp when 'studying any past period' (1965: 63). The structure of feminist feeling captured by Churchill in the period of second-wave feminism – its socialist character and ecological dimension – is explored in Section 1 as I feel-think my way back to three of her plays: *Owners* (1972), *Vinegar Tom* (1976), and *Light Shining in Buckinghamshire* (1976). On the one hand, these works evince different forms, techniques, tones, or themes; on the other, common to all three is a 'felt sense' of the patriarchal and capitalist structures that ignited women's affectively and experientially realised attachments to feminism. Together, they attest to a new structure of feminist feeling in British theatre and augur Churchill's seminal role in the forging of a feminist-theatre tradition. Moreover, analysis of these works, as well as those explored elsewhere in the Element, evidences how Churchill excels at *feeling structures*. By this I mean her unsurpassed capacity among contemporary British dramatists to innovate dramatic elements, the deployment, combinations, or arrangements of which have the potential to yield affectively realised, politicising responses to the subject in hand.

1.1 Introducing the Socialist Character of Churchill's Feminism: *Owners*

'For years and years' Churchill thought of herself 'as a writer before [she] thought of [herself] as a woman', but in the 1970s she came to identify as a 'feminist writer' (qtd in McFerran 1977: 13). The 'feminist position' that she began to sense 'quite strongly' arose out of her increased experience of 'situations which involve[d] women' (qtd in McFerran 1977: 13). Acknowledging her growing attachments to a 'feminist position' as one that 'inevitably' came into her writing, Churchill nonetheless was clear that she was not using her plays as vehicles for feminism: she did not see herself as a 'feminist using writing to advance that position' (qtd in McFerran 1977: 13). What can be said of her writing in this period is that there is an affinity between or resonance with the second-wave feminist movement and the feminist outlook inscribed in her plays. Churchill observed that 'one of the things the Women's Movement has done is to show the way the [inequality] traps work' (qtd in McFerran 1977: 13). My observation is that her theatre similarly is charged with a creatively rendered capacity to demonstrate how those 'traps work'.

Working out how women were ensnared by patriarchy was a fundamental concern of second-wave feminism. 'Patriarchal attitudes', to borrow the title of Eva Figes' classic feminist text that Churchill was reading at the time of writing *Owners*, came to be widely understood as consolidating and upholding the centuries-old tradition of male supremacy responsible for women's subordination. Women drawn to and engaged in radical-feminist politics and activism spearheaded the revolt against patriarchalism. A radical-feminist imaginary was revolutionary in outlook: it demanded the end to patriarchy that reformist strategies alone could not dismantle. As Figes explained in terms and tones typical of feminist writing at the time: 'Social reform does not necessarily mean a change of attitude, and the last citadel that a man will ever concede is the idea of his own superiority' (1978: 22).

The patriarchal trap emerged as no less a concern for those women on the Left whose idea of a socially progressive future was rooted in socialism. However, an immediate, pressing issue was how to reconcile a gender-blind, socialist tradition with emergent feminist attentions to women's oppression. Ultimately, this necessitated feminist revisions to, rather than abandonment of, socialist analysis of class and economic relations under capitalism: critical attentions to class, economics, *and* gender[2] were necessary to explanations of and demand for the revolutionary transformation of women's dual exploitation in the patriarchal home/family and capitalist workplace.

On the one hand aware that 'socialism and feminism aren't synonymous' and on the other 'fee[ing] strongly about both', Churchill explained that she 'wouldn't be interested in a form of one that didn't include the other' (qtd in Betsko & Koenig 1987: 78). With its fusion of *anti*-patriarchal attitudes and objections to private property, *Owners*, which premiered in 1972 at the Royal Court Theatre, finds Churchill forming a 'feminist position' that includes rather than excludes socialist dynamics. The production marks the beginning of her long and enduring association with the Court and the second phase of her writing career devoted chiefly to the stage. This was in contrast to her previous work that throughout the 1960s had been mainly for radio. For the purpose of this present discussion, *Owners* provides an initial window into the socialist character of Churchill's feminism.

The play was inspired by her first-hand encounters with tenants facing eviction at the hands of unscrupulous landlords and property developers in her London Borough of Islington, and a more abstract idea relating to the juxtaposition of a Zen-like passivity with a Western mode of owning and achieving. With its main protagonists consisting of a quartet of two couples – Marion and Clegg, Lisa and Alec – and a fifth character, Worsely, acting as a go-between, *Owners* presents the power of owning and the abject state of being owned to dizzying, stupefying effect. With its Ortonesque-inflected dark-comedic register, the play dislocates owning as the norm for a Western way of life, rendering it absurd if not pathological.

Anti-patriarchal feelings are structured through the depiction of Clegg. A butcher by trade, Clegg harbours murderous intentions towards Marion and views all women as meat. His patriarchal authority is under threat: his property-developer wife is more successful in business (Clegg's butcher's shop has failed) and eludes his control. It is not feminist polemic that expresses what were then women's widely felt discontents with an injurious system of patriarchal privilege, but Churchill's dark-comedic rendering of Clegg that exposes the absurdity of 'patriarchal attitudes' from a feminist perspective. There is a somewhat vaudevillian feel to the exchanges between Clegg and the allegiance-switching Worsely (Marion's property enforcer, but also Clegg's henchman). They act like a comedy duo whose jokes always pivot to murder: when Clegg boasts of having killed a man while serving in the army, Worsely asks if it was 'one of the enemy'. 'It was a guerilla', Clegg explains; 'You were claiming just now it was a man', objects

---

[2] The initial conjugation of class and gender would subsequently extend to race and sexuality.

Worsely (Churchill 1985: 37). Moreover, Worsely who wants to cheat life by killing himself, something he repeatedly fails to do given that he is so 'safety prone' (Churchill 1985: 10), parodically exposes patriarchy's investment in cheating death through a father-to-son lineage. As Clegg ruefully reflects when his butcher's shop fails: 'now I've no business I don't need a son. Having no son I don't need a business' (Churchill 1985: 9).

For all the play's anti-patriarchal feelings, it is the socialist-inflected objections to the idea of owning that are paramount. A democracy built on private ownership is no democracy at all is the feeling *Owners* transmits as it shows the traps of owning things, property, and people. Marion is the epicentre of what Churchill referred to as 'western capitalistic individualism' (qtd in Gooch 1973: i) – a woman possessed by an acquisitive zeal, puritanical in her belief that 'God helps those who helps themselves' (Figes 1978: 79). It is unexpected: a woman not a man who divines life's purpose as one of capitalist achievement – a gender-reversal technique to heighten a critical sensing of capitalism's masculinist imagination. In another way, it also gestures to the socio-economic inequalities perpetuated by the likes of Marion, the high-achieving, individual woman whose material gain comes at the expense of those women (and men) trapped in poverty. Where Marion gains, down-trodden, working mum Lisa loses. First, it is Lisa's things (she is burgled), then it is her home (she faces eviction), her husband (Marion wants to re-possess Alec with whom she had a former relationship), and her baby (signed over to Clegg in a fit of post-natal depression). Feel-see what 'individualistic capitalism' looks like Churchill urges as she renders the absurdity of capitalist 'attitudes' and their power to dispossess.

The Zen-like Alec, who, in a passive, depressive, "feminine" state, has given up on wanting anything, is a further means by which Churchill impresses a *dis*-identification with owning. By not wanting, choosing, or acting on anything, what Alec *does* is to frustrate the desire to own. The capacity of his passive resistance to frustrate a belief in owning comes to the fore in his encounters with Marion. In filmed extracts from Act 1, Scene 5 created for BBC One's *The Caryl Churchill Omnibus* (1988),[3] Maggie Steed as Marion verbally and physically dominates the space (Alec and Lisa's shabby apartment). Actor Nigel Terry depicts Alec in an affectless state of self-containment, relaxed and lying on a single bed. Only when responding to his senile mother (Tricia Kelly) does he react with alacrity, moving to adjust her chair, attending to her comfort – a *felt*

---

[3] The Omnibus is available to UK-based students and teachers in schools and universities on the Educational Recording Agency's (ERA's) Video Streaming Platform: https://era.org.uk/lit-resource/omnibus-caryl-churchill/.

response that Marion's entreaties singularly fail to elicit. A smiling Steed bargains ('Two thousand pounds to get out of my house') and cajoles ('For Lisa's sake. For your sons') (Churchill 1985: 29). Thereafter, as she delivers an extract from Marion's 'Onward Christian soldiers' speech (Churchill 1985: 30), Steed towers above and looks down on Terry now seated on a chair, contemplating an orange. Close-up shots of Steed's facial expressions bring the emotional drive of her acquisitiveness firmly into focus – her face all the more animated, her speech infused with an energetic zeal 'to get better, be best' (Churchill 1985: 30). Her eyes light up as she speaks of 'the animals [that] are ours. The vegetables and minerals. For us to consume' – with an emphasis on the verb 'to consume' (Churchill 1985: 30). There's guilt in consuming, in achieving, but it is outstripped by the stress Steed/Marion places on the word 'progress'. She knows there are 'children with no shoes and socks in the houses' she buys, but that 'gritty lump' of guilty feeling embedded in the 'pearl' of ownership will not prevent Marion from working 'like a dog' to "succeed" (Churchill 1985: 30). As Steed closes with the line 'Most women are the fleas but I'm the dog', her delivery accenting the word 'dog' (Churchill 1985: 30), the filmed extract segues to archival footage of a triumphant, prime ministerial Margaret Thatcher outside No. 10 Downing Street. It is an associative link that renders Marion the harbinger of the masculinist, capitalist, Thatcherite drive to private ownership in the decade to come.

'Emotional capitalism' was the term that the play's director Nicholas Wright used to describe *Owners* (Gooch 1973: i). This is an insightful description since it touches on the idea that the workings of capitalism, like those of any political system, require an emotional investment. To secure and maintain a hegemonic position, capitalism has to work at a political, economic, *and* emotional level: it has to shape and fulfil peoples' wants, desires, and needs in order to prevent them from desiring and choosing an alternative system. Alec, in his affectless state of not wanting and not consuming (note he contemplates but not eats the orange), is devoid of an emotional investment in capitalism. At the close of the play when he returns to feeling and working again, it is with an altruistic outlook. He risks and loses his life while trying to rescue a neighbour's baby in a house fire ordered by Marion and set by Worsely. Hence, a feeling for a selfless, care-giving order disappears as it appears – the ghost of a future that might have been.

1.2 'Speaking Bitterness': *Vinegar Tom*

With its absurdist strains and dark-comedic antics, *Owners* eschews allegiance to British theatre's historically dominant realist tradition. 'None of the characters are particularly realistic', Churchill explained; even Lisa's 'more naturalistically written' role is 'exaggerated' to a degree that distorts, defamiliarizes, a sense of everyday owning – 'my house, my husband, my children, my family' (qtd in Gooch 1973: i).

Churchill was not alone in parting company with realism; feminist dramatists and practitioners increasingly rejected realism's representational apparatus. As Jill Dolan explained, from a feminist perspective realism was deemed 'a conservative force that reproduces and reinforces dominant cultural relations'; its traditional form and patriarchal tendencies were perceived as limiting and oppressive to the representation of women (Dolan 1988: 84).[4] Although realism was by no means lacking a critical dimension, as evinced in its modus operandi of representing the individual who comes to recognise an unjust society, under feminist scrutiny its political efficacy as a dramatic form appeared inadequate to the task of revolutionary consciousness-raising. Its emotional attachment to the individual's struggle and their ultimate entrapment in a society whose values are upheld rather than changed, diminishes a capacity to see-think the workings of oppressive structures and their reversible rather than immutable character. This begins to explain the Brechtian turn in socialist-feminist theatre-making where a reprise of the A-effect, *Gestus*, or historicization is fused with critical attentions to gender and class, patriarchal and capitalist traps (Reinelt 1994; Diamond 1997). Churchill's own Brechtian-inflected presentational rather than representational apparatus evolves through her phase of collaborating with the companies Monstrous Regiment and Joint Stock.

More than any other play by Churchill in the 1970s, it is *Vinegar Tom* that captures the feminist wave of personal-to-political feeling, hence its central position in this section. There are three primary, interconnecting ways through which analysis of the play affords us a felt sense of the decade's feminist revolutionary consciousness: by understanding the feminist collaboration between Churchill and Monstrous Regiment that underpinned its original production; recognising its depiction of witchcraft as a crucible of feminist anger; and attending to the Brechtian elements that structure its revolutionary rhythms of socialist feminism.

The 'patriarchal attitudes' that feminists experienced in the socialist movement at large – in its political groups, organisations, or trade unions – were mirrored in the left-wing, alternative, political theatre companies that burgeoned in the 1970s. Hence the reason why in 1975 feminist theatre makers Chris Bowler, Gillian Hanna, and Mary McCusker founded Monstrous Regiment as a collective with a majority of women. Akin to

---

[4] For further discussion of realism and feminist perspectives, see Aston 2016.

Churchill, the Monsters, as they were affectionately called, saw themselves first and foremost as theatre makers who brought a political perspective to their work, rather than as a 'group of politically-motivated women who wanted to use theatre as a means of expressing [their] politics' (Hanna 1989: 49). Also, like Churchill, their political perspective embraced socialism and feminism; in their formative years (and beyond), as Hanna explained, they were working out how these 'two sides' of their politics could be combined (Hanna 1989: 48). Ultimately their experience of founding the company was inseparably linked with a feeling of being part of a 'much bigger' feminist picture – the 'exhilarating' sense of wanting 'to change the world', of being 'part of a huge wave of women' who 'were going to remake everything' (Hanna 1991: xxix).

To be 'part of a huge wave of women' wanting 'to remake everything', was to be caught up in a feminist wave of anger – a deeply felt 'fury' that 'was about everything' (Hanna 1989: 50). This was not then an isolated angry response to this or that issue of equality, but a rage-filled response to inequalities and injustices that were endemic in women's everyday lives – not one thing, but 'everything'. And in the subject of witchcraft, Churchill and Monstrous Regiment found a crucible for women's explosive anger forged over centuries of oppression – the persecution of women not for being witches, but quite simply for being women. It was a topic of mutual interest; Churchill and the Monsters shared reading and ideas in a process and structure not dissimilar to the consciousness-raising groups of the women's movement. They got together as a small group of collectively organised women sharing and working out their 'ideas and feelings' (Monstrous Regiment 1982: 41).

In *Woman's Estate*, Juliet Mitchell observed the prejudice that occurs when it is women who gather together to talk: the critics who dismissed 'consciousness-raising sessions as "group therapy"', or as a covert way of maligning and chastising women for 'moaning again, gossiping their complaints, having a nag' (1971: 61–62). Hence, to counter this prejudicial view, Mitchell drew a parallel between women's consciousness-raising and the 'Chinese revolutionary practice of "speaking bitterness"' (1971: 62). It was not a direct parallel since the two contexts were radically different, but the salient observation she made in making the comparison was that:

> The first symptom of oppression is the repression of words; the state of suffering is so total and so assumed that it is not known to be there. 'Speaking bitterness' is the bringing to consciousness of the virtually unconscious oppression; one person's realization of an injustice brings to mind other injustices for the whole group.' (1971: 62)

In *Vinegar Tom's* seventeenth-century setting, 'speaking bitterness' is the preserve of unruly women: the cunning woman, Ellen, whose healing powers contravene male, medical authority; the single mother, Alice, who, like her aged mother Joan, is not bound to a husband. All these women are poor but pose a threat to the social order as they disturb, violate gender norms. And then there are the women at risk of becoming outcasts: middle-class Betty, locked up because she refuses to marry; Susan, married with children, but reluctantly seeking an abortion for another, unwanted pregnancy. The 'state of suffering' each of them experiences varies from woman to woman: Alice cursed, abused, or assaulted by male lovers (Scenes 1 & 13); Betty bled and "treated" as a hysteric by the doctor (Scene 6); Susan consumed by grief and guilt after the abortion (Scene 13); Joan and Ellen, the old and the wise, hanged as witches (Scene 19). Equally, altered personal-to-political states of perception also vary from Susan's misguided sense that she must be a sinner and a witch, through Betty's awareness that her happiness depends on escaping medical/marital authority, to Alice's belated realisation that she should have trusted in Ellen's "cunning" ways. After her mother and Ellen are hanged in the public square, Alice voices her if-only yearning to be the witch she never was: 'If I could live I'd be a witch now after what they've done. I'd make wax men and melt them on a slow fire. I'd kill their animals and blast their crops and make such storms, I'd wreck their ships all over the world' (Churchill 1985: 175).

If, as Mitchell observes, the 'first symptom of oppression is the repression of words', an attendant difficulty is created by the phallocentric ownership of language that is resistant to naming women's oppression, putting into words, the 'suffering' which has been 'hidden far from consciousness'. Recollect, for instance, Betty Friedan's 'unspoken' 'problem that has no name' as she explored the unnamed experience of women's lives confined to post-war domesticity (2010: 5). In *Vinegar Tom* the meanings of words prove decidedly slippery. Betty yearns to escape, to fly away from the marital life she is destined for, but flying is what witches do. Women are condemned by whichever words they speak. Alice can deny her boy is the devil's son, but if he is not, then the child can speak against her; either way she can be denounced as a witch. In short, endorsed by the "Christian" church, the legal and medical authorities, phallocentric language excels at 'speaking *patriarchal* bitterness' against women. Furthermore, as in *Owners* with its depiction of Marion as the egregious property developer, *Vinegar Tom* demonstrates that women may also be complicit in upholding the masculinist imagination in thought, deed, or word – witchfinder Packer's assistant, the ironically named Goody, who profits from the business of searching out witches; Margery who scapegoats Joan for all the troubles at her farm, the failed crops and dying cows.

Where the unruly, seventeenth-century women struggle to diagnose their condition, the songs that Churchill wrote to be delivered out of character pulsate with the rhythms of a contemporary feminist consciousness. These are, as it were, the songs of women's liberation. Well-versed in anti-patriarchal sentiments, they speak the unspoken truths that 'Nobody Sings' about: women's reproductive bodies that menstruate and dry up with age (Churchill 1985: 141–142); wombs scrutinised by the doctor's 'metal eye' (Churchill 1985: 150); women seen as sexual and sinful in a 'dirty-boy' gaze (Churchill 1985: 179). Where the first song, 'Nobody Sings', refers to one woman's objection to her invisibility as 'whispered in a rage' (Churchill 1985: 142), it is women's collectively felt antipathy towards male domination and control that builds over the course of all seven songs.

Recordings of the songs are archived on Monstrous Regiment's website.[5] You can either listen to them in sequence or hear extracts played against a montage of black and white images of the production. These archival traces capture the dark tones of the play's original staging: the image of Joan/Mary McCusker cloaked in rags (poverty) sitting on a wooden pallet that serves as a bed; or Alice/Gillian Hanna depicted in a tableau of abject terror – seated, her hands bound, eyes and mouth wide open, witchfinder Packer/Roger Allam's controlling hand resting on her head. And all the while, Helen Glavin's musical compositions for the piano track the sounds of women's oppression as archaic *and* contemporary.

After listening to the songs, I came away with a heightened sense of how Churchill's lyrics are punctuated with points of feminist-political explanation. Look at how the nation demands a puritanical work ethic and women's subordination in the patriarchally conceived family. Glavin choruses in 'If Everybody Worked as Hard as Me', hitting a satirical note at the piano, an act/song highly reminiscent of British comedienne Victoria Wood. Or see how the masculinist imagination projects the image of women as evil, the entire cast collectively urge as they sing the show's up-tempo, final number ('Evil Women').

All told; by explaining and commenting on the past persecution of women from the vantage point of the present, the songs invite us to understand the historical forces that denied women an alternative future and how those forces have their contemporary equivalents. Theatre critics in the main were far less well disposed to the music than they were to the dramatic scenes – were more drawn to the past, not seeing the need for the songs' present-day parallels and interventions.[6] But it is the feeling structures of the songs and the scenes

---

[5] Home– Monstrous Regiment.
[6] Monstrous Regiment's website includes a collection of the reviews: Vinegar-Tom-1976-Words-1-Reviews.pdf (monstrousregiment.co.uk)

together that create a Brechtian mode of seeing history haunted by what might have been (Betty gets to fly away, or Alice leaves for a big city and takes lovers when she wants) and what needs to change in the present.

Elsewhere I have termed this a mode of double-eye viewing, positing Churchill's deployment of Brechtian conventions and techniques as valuable to resisting a one-eyed view of the world in which events, past or present, are seen as inevitable or unchangeable (2025: 284).[7] With its sung observational commentary, series of episodic scenes, ensemble of characters, and estrangement of past–present structures of oppression, *Vinegar Tom* is firmly rooted in the Brechtian terrain. In this aesthetic, 'patriarchal *attitudes*' are forged by means of the social *Gestus*. For instance, when Alice, half-strangled by Jack, is forced to place her hand between his thighs to "treat" his phantasmal castration, her action gestures to the threat women's sexuality poses to patriarchy. And when women from the cast play Kramer and Sprenger, speaking 'genuine' lines from the *Malleus Maleficarum: The Hammer of Witches* in the style of 'music hall gents' (Churchill 1985: 134), the scene points to the gendered power relations between persecutor and persecuted, its dark-comedic, gender-bending antics subjecting patriarchal authority to ridicule.

Patriarchalism is also linked to the economic structures that consign the likes of Alice and Joan to poverty. Joan may be 'glad' that her husband who used to beat her is dead but, as she wryly observes, with a man to provide for them 'We'd have more to eat' (Churchill 1985: 141). Hence Churchill's socialist-feminist eye sees how patriarchy and poverty structure Alice and Joan's circumstances; neither woman is a witch, their only "crime" is to be husbandless and poor. Only Ellen has a skill that enables her to live independently of men – the skill of healing that she refuses to turn into an economic transaction, instead relying on whatever little gifts people choose to leave her. Her restorative powers are freely given to all those who come to her door. In brief, it is through the depiction of Ellen's altruistic care-giving that Churchill counterpoints an acquisitive puritanism and its devaluation of all those it leaves behind. As Barbara Ehrenreich and Deirdre English observe in *Witches, Midwives, and Nurses* that Churchill and Monstrous Regiment consulted when researching witchcraft, it was the woman healer who 'held out the hope of change in this world' (1973: 15).

If that was then, what is it that is stopping you now? This is the question poignantly posed by Glavin and Josefina Cupido in the song 'Lament for the Witches', a lamentation rhythmically structured to the beat of Cupido's drums.

---

[7] My descriptor of theatre's double eye is indebted to Richard Hoggart's working-class-orientated perspective on the necessity and difficulty of bringing the double eye of the personal and the political into focus.

It is a question that was core to the feminist movement, raised and addressed in its consciousness-raising groups. Expressed through the medium of theatre, it begs a related question: what role does theatre play in political struggles committed to alternative futures? When feminist theatre-making contemporaneously pursues similar lines of enquiry to those of the feminist movement at large, it helps, as Hanna observed, 'to open a door' to questions women are already asking (1989: 50). Political theatre rooted in identity politics has often been criticised for preaching to the converted. But this negates seeing theatre as a communal space in which to wrestle with, work out, political questions, ideas, and feelings. Critical reactions from women to Monstrous Regiment's politics (see Monstrous Regiment 1982: 42) suggest not a homogenous body of converts, but a heterogenous mix of spectators working out points of identification or dis-identification with the play's socialist-feminist dynamics.

Heterogeneous rather than homogeneous, the feminist movement nonetheless generated women's widely shared, personal-to-political feeling that it was possible for them to change the world. But for that to happen, it was necessary for a revolutionary feminist consciousness to 'move from the individual, to the small group, *to the whole society*' (Mitchell 1971: 63; emphasis added).

1.3 'A Revolution That Didn't Happen': *Light Shining in Buckinghamshire*

It is *Light Shining in Buckinghamshire* (hereafter abbreviated to *Light Shining*) that structures a feeling for a 'whole society' in the grips of a revolutionary fever as Churchill depicts England's seventeenth-century civil war and utopian yearnings for heaven on earth. God's army of men turned soldiers fight for their freedom, which in political terms translates into the demand to expand voting rights – to have a parliament representative of and chosen by the people. Power changes hands from the monarchy to Oliver Cromwell's parliament men, and the nation is poised to revolutionise its old ways. But the Putney Debates that close the first of the play's two acts evince Cromwell's parliament rejecting the people's proposals, committed as it is to maintain property rights. An 'eye to property' and the fear that equal voting rights will by extension lead to the idea of an equal share in property – 'a freedom to the land, to take the ground, to till it' – defeats the future that could have been (Churchill 1985: 213). As the ghost of the future that never happened in *What If If Only* admonishes, 'stupid stupid kept choosing the wrong things and let me die' (Churchill 2021: 9).

At the time of *Owners*, Churchill explained that 'on a simple political level I think owning is stupid. It would be better to have land nationalised' (qtd in Gooch 1973: i). The idea of a democracy built on private ownership that she scrutinised in her earlier play is re-viewed through *Light Shining*'s critical sensing 'of a revolution that didn't happen' (Churchill 1985: 183). Like *Vinegar Tom,* the play invites us to see through the received version of history with an eye to contemporary inequalities. Created with and for the alternative theatre company Joint Stock, *Light Shining* also draws on Brechtian conventions and techniques: big events are reported rather than enacted; scenes are not formed as part of a story but presented as episodic fragments, each with a title and social attitude to the incident it presents. Performing as a democratic ensemble, the Joint Stock actors, in accordance with Churchill's instructions, eschewed the convention of playing the same character throughout (Churchill 1985: 184). As an actor plays a character in one scene, but a different performer takes over the role in another, the habit of watching how individuals progress through time-bound, plotted action comes undone. In *Light Shining*, what Churchill's Brechtian double eye views with objectivity is the making and unmaking of a revolution – a socially orientated eye that sees how each discrete event hangs together in the telling of a revolution that ultimately 'didn't happen'.

The play's feminist spectator sees how the concept of the people deployed by the Levellers in the Putney Debates, as they advocate for the rights of the common *man*,[8] excludes women. Put *Vinegar Tom* side by side with *Light Shining* – two halves of the same patriarchal coin – and it is not hard to see why. The patriarchal control and persecution of women in the former shadows the power-brokering debates in the latter. In *Light Shining* it is men who judge a woman for begging (she is whipped) and the male authority of the church that silences a woman for preaching (she is beaten). Thus, Churchill demonstrates that 'a freedom to the land' and women's freedom are both critical to democratic futures. It is in the linkage between women's rights and the right to common land that an ecological dimension to her socialist-feminism becomes palpable.

Links between ecology and feminism were only just emerging in the 1970s. French critic and activist Françoise d'Eaubonne is credited with coining the term 'ecofeminism' in *Le féminisme ou la mort/ Feminism or Death* published in 1974, and translated into English in 2022.[9] In the latter, d'Eaubonne launched a savage critique of patriarchy – one echoed by Churchill in her structures of anti-patriarchal feeling rendered in all three plays considered here. However,

---

[8] The political movement of the Levellers championed the extension of suffrage, parliamentary reform, and religious freedom.

[9] D'Eaubonne was a radical voice in the 1970s wave of 'new French feminisms' (Marks & de Courtivron: 1981); in 1972 she founded the centre for *Ecologie-Féminisme*. The long overdue translation of *Le féminisme ou la mort* into English finally allows an international readership access to her pioneering ecofeminist philosophy and politics.

unlike Churchill, d'Eaubonne rejected socialism, arguing that it shared capitalism's machismo; both systems create scenes of ecological disaster, she argued, because both are governed by phallocracy. No revolution that is in the hands of men succeeds because 'none has ever gone further than replacing one regime by another, one system by another in accordance with the existing structures' (2022: 214). *Light Shining's* failed revolution attests to this observation, but contrastingly, Churchill does not abandon socialism. The socialist-feminist lens she turns on *Light Shining's* revolutionary struggles juxtaposed with scenes of women's oppression impresses the need for a *feminist* socialism. Thus, where d'Eaubonne's first use of the term ecofeminism adjectivally attaches eco to feminism, Churchill's theatre calls for the triangulation of ecology, socialism, and feminism.

It is important to notice this triangulation since it distinguishes Churchill's stance from strains of emergent radical-feminist thinking in which environmentalist and feminist concerns also begin to connect through the recognition of man's treatment of women and the earth. For instance, Mary Daly's *Gyn/Ecology* (1978) and Susan Griffin's *Women and Nature* (1978) are books whose titles gesture to a special link between women and the natural environment; their contents critique patriarchal ownership of women and nature. However, Churchill does not subscribe to an eco-radical-feminist vision in which women are accorded power over men and the earth.[10] From her socialist-feminist standpoint, she demonstrates that a utopian 'world upside down' is dependent not only on overturning patriarchal power, but also on dismantling capitalist systems of economic maldistribution and their power to deny 'the use of the earth' for the 'nourishment' of all people (Churchill 1985: 219).

Light Shining's second act sees the common land that could have been used to sustain those living in poverty enclosed; the Diggers fail in their attempts to reclaim the earth that is destined not to nourish but to make a profit.[11] The landlord Star, formerly a recruiting officer for God's army, claims to be introducing a better style of management, but this is only the old, socially hierarchical way masquerading as the new. And meanwhile, a disbanded army reunites as a colonialist force against Ireland: the English army will ironically fight against the Irish people's struggle for rights, the very cause the soldiers previously took up arms for.

---

[10] In this regard, d'Eaubonne similarly eschews the idea of women taking power. Instead, she posits the 'feminine' as a system of 'non-power' in which 'the human being will finally be treated first as a person, and not above all else as a male or female' (2022: 222).

[11] Diggers adopted the practice of claiming and digging common land to aid the poor.

Where a revolutionary consciousness lingers is in the group of Ranters[12] whose meeting at the close of the act/play balances the Putney Debates at the end of the first. This is a rather different assembly to those all-female consciousness-raising groups in the women's liberation movement: a coming together of women *and* men trying to make sense of their experiences. They know they have been cheated and lied to by the rich, the army, the parliament, and the church. They make their own kind of "church": drink and blaspheme; 'speak bitterness' against anti-democratic powers; mourn the Levellers killed in the struggles; contemplate whether Christ, the redeemer, will still come, or whether his spirit is already among them. All are free to speak, women included. No one is judged, punished, or cast out; what they have, they share. And their idea of holding 'all goods in common' encompasses their 'bodies' (Churchill 1985: 234) – a desire for sexual freedom that Churchill will go on to explore in her next Joint Stock collaboration, *Cloud Nine* (see Section 4).

Light Shining has had numerous revivals, including two at the Royal National Theatre, London, both in General Election years: the first in 1997 that saw Tony Blair's New Labour government elected; the second in 2015, the year that returned David Cameron as prime minister and leader of the Conservative Party. Around the time of the play's original production, Churchill felt that 'the thousands of men and women who tried to change their lives' back in the seventeenth-century had 'voices' that were 'surprisingly close to us' (1985: 183); the same observation could be made of the two high-profile revivals, twenty years and near on forty years later. In 1997 it was the land rights movement that, akin to the seventeenth-century Diggers, was determined on 'Turning the World Upside Down' as campaigner George Monbiot explained (1997). And socialist journalist Paul Foot noted the parallel between the play's depiction of parliament's betrayal of the people and Blair's soon-to-be-government 'abjectly surrendering economic power to the people who already have it, and, in the process, polluting the political power they seek from the votes of people most of whom have no wealth at all' (qtd in Aston 2010: 105). To hear the Putney Debates again in the 2015 production against the political backdrop of Cameron's austerity Britain was also to be reminded of the nation's past and present failures to democratise. As theatre critic Kate Kellaway headlined: 'There is no mystery about the National's pre-election scheduling: this is a play about protest [. . .] It highlights the continuing reasons for ranting in modern Britain – most of all the unclosed gap between rich and poor' (2015). To mark that increasing 'gap', director Lyndsey Turner and designer Es Devlin

---

[12] Ranters refused to recognise the authority of the church; they believed in economic and sexual freedoms.

created an overall Brechtian *Gestus*: the National's Lyttleton stage was first set as a lavish banqueting scene, the entire stage serving as a table for a host of wealthy guests. Thereafter, it was gradually divested of its rich trappings, ceding the space to those too poor to be seated at the table.[13]

I saw the 2015 revival in the context of participating in the National's panel on Churchill,[14] delivering a presentation that involved members from the cast of *Light Shining* reading extracts from her work. The extract I selected from *Light Shining* was a scene from the first act, 'Two Women Look in a Mirror' (Churchill 1985: 207). What makes this scene so memorable is the way in which Churchill distils an epic (in the dual sense) moment of socialist-feminist reflection into this brief episode as two poor women see themselves for the first time in a broken mirror looted from the house of a nobleman. It is only by appropriating the gaze of the dispossessed aristocrat that the women are able to see themselves. By taking his goods and redistributing them among themselves; by taking the corn that is rightfully theirs; by pulling down the pictures of the landowning, patriarchal class, they glimpse a utopian 'world upside down'. Land, property and wealth redistributed; women no longer excluded and exploited on the basis of their gender and class. This is Churchill's eco-socialist-feminist vision: 'Equality and cake and no bad bits at all' (Churchill 2021: 10).

What happens to Churchill's vision for an egalitarian and sustainable future in a political climate increasingly hostile to feminism and socialism, and how she impresses the need to see the world could still be turned upside down are matters core to Section 2.

2 Against 'The Great Moving Right Show'

There is a moment in *The Caryl Churchill Omnibus* when the playwright appears to be lost for words. Asked why she was drawn to the Left rather than the Right, Churchill hesitates, smiles, then jokes, 'because the Left was right' (BBC: 1988). I have always been struck by this instance of momentary bewilderment since it expresses Churchill's feeling that the question hardly needs to be asked. As she subsequently elaborates, it is 'obvious to be concerned and to feel that it was wrong that one lot of people were less well off than another, or that people were colonised' (BBC: 1988).

---

[13] With its large cast and extravagant design, Turner's production represented a significant departure from the original Joint Stock production and director Mark Wing-Davey's 1997 revival. These were both touring productions that opted for a minimalist staging and a cast of just six performers. For details of Wing-Davey's revival that toured between 1996 and 1997 see Aston 2010: 104–106.

[14] 'Caryl Churchill in Context', 26 May 2015.

However, for Churchill and all those on the Left, an increasing problem going into the 1980s was the UK's dramatic 'swing to the right' – the advent of what the Gramscian-inspired cultural theorist Stuart Hall termed 'The Great Moving Right Show' (1988: 39). As Hall explained in *The Hard Road to Renewal*, although the gradual disarticulation of the Left dated back to the late 1960s,[15] it was 'the political project of "Thatcherism"' that accelerated and produced its 'crisis' (1988: 1). To address that 'crisis' necessitated the Left's critique of Thatcherism and strategies for 'renewal'. Seminal to the latter was the need to re-think the 'soil in which socialism takes root' (1988: 181): to embrace not only the working-class struggle but the social struggles occurring on multiple fronts, including feminism.

As Section 1 established, a political linkage between feminism and socialism was fundamental to Churchill's conception of socially progressive futures. What happens when feminism *loses* its socialist dimension is a concern she raises in her seminal play *Top Girls* (1982). Re-viewing *Top Girls*, I focus on Churchill's critique of feminism's own 'moving right show' and the loss of socialist-feminist feeling this portends. Thereafter, elucidating the eco-socialist-feminist aesthetic of *Fen* (1983) – a play in which feminism is literally rooted in the 'soil' of socialism – my analysis reveals how Churchill signals feminist and ecologically aware strategies for the renewal of a socialist left. The Section concludes by looking to the mid-1990s – to the dark fairy magic of *The Skriker* (1994), where the failure to cancel the long-running 'Great Moving Right Show' is proven to have deadly social and ecological consequences.

2.1 'Iron Ladies' and Feeling the Loss of Socialism: *Top Girls*

On 26 July 1982, one month before the opening of Churchill's *Top Girls* at the Royal Court Theatre (28 August 1982), Margaret Thatcher gave the first memorial lecture in honour of Dame Margery Corbett-Ashby (1882–1981), a seminal figure in the women's suffrage movement. Entitled 'Women in a Changing World', Thatcher's lecture was both an homage to 'Dame Margery [and] her great contributions to the century of change', and an opportunity to reflect on women's position in the present (Thatcher: 1982). Paradoxically, given Corbett-Ashby's support of women's rights, Thatcher declared her hostility to the women's movement:

> The battle for women's rights has been largely won. The days when they were demanded and discussed in strident tones should be gone forever. And I hope they are. I hated those strident tones that you still hear from some Women's Libbers'. (Thatcher: 1982)

---

[15] For details see Hall, 'The Great Moving Right Show', 1988: 39–56.

Hence, in one 'strident' swipe, Thatcher dismissed feminism's historic second wave as a redundant, unwelcome malingerer.

By contrast, *Top Girls* finds Churchill pursuing and exploring the fortunes of feminism in a changing nation whose political pendulum is firmly swinging to the right. The play was not workshopped; ideas for *Top Girls* germinated over a long period of time. As Churchill summarised, her different 'starting points' included: a 'floating idea' of women from the past having coffee with a woman from the present; Thatcher's election and whether this was a positive thing because she was a woman, or detrimental because she was a Conservative; concern about the way women's corporate advancement in North America was viewed as feminist success; and the idea of two sisters one of whom stayed put while the other left in an attempt to change her life (BBC: 1988). Woven together, these ideas ultimately structure a socialist-feminist critique of top-girl, Thatcherite ideology.

The opening restaurant scene that developed from the 'floating idea' establishes Marlene in a genealogy of exceptional women; her guests are Isabella Bird, Lady Nijo, Dull Gret, Pope Joan and Patient Griselda. What they have 'in common' is 'activity' (Churchill 1990a: 60); with the exception of the all-too-patient Griselda, Marion from *Owners* would certainly recognise the women as kindred spirits. But it is a commonality that has none of the 1970s consciousness-raising, personal-is-political ethos. When one woman speaks about a life-changing event, another often responds with a detail about her *own* life, rather than engaging with the experience that has been shared. Hence, the dinner-table conversation is less of an exchange and more a series of interrupted monologues, formally rendered through Churchill's pioneering use of overlapping dialogue, thereby underscoring the idea that while the women talk, they rarely *listen*. Moreover, recognition of a political dimension to their personal experiences – the instances of patriarchal power in the form of controlling fathers or abusive husbands that seep through the autobiographical tales – remains notably absent. It is only at the close of the act that the hitherto repressed dissonance between their 'extraordinary achievements' (Churchill 1990a: 67) and the discriminations or oppressions they faced truly explodes: Marlene's celebratory dinner ends in chaotic, drunken, angry weeping.

As a modern-day incarnation of a powerful woman, Marlene is not one of the 'Women's Libbers'' Thatcher despised. Rather she belongs to the ranks of what Beatrix Campbell describes as the Tory-voting 'iron ladies' (1987). 'She's a tough lady, Maggie,' Marlene declares – a woman who 'certainly' has her 'vote' (Churchill 1990a: 138). 'Tough' is an unexpected attribute for a 'lady'. But as Campbell elucidates, the UK's then most powerful woman was 'a model neither of traditional femininity nor feminism': the image of 'female power' she projected was based on combining 'patriarchal and feminine discourses' (1987: 246). This endorsement of the 'patriarchal' and the 'feminine' ultimately signifies Thatcher's key objective: 'to be a woman who does what men do' (1987: 241). This too is Marlene's aspiration. In the employment agency scenes depicted in Act Two, she and her other 'iron-lady' operatives, Nell and Win, have the power to decide on people's future employment prospects. Any woman they interview ideally needs to be, as Nell puts it, a 'Tough bird like us' (Churchill 1990a: 102).

Not all of Thatcher's 'iron ladies' were exceptional women like Marlene. Indeed, it was the figure of the stay-at-home housewife that Thatcher primarily courted as she invoked good housekeeping as the recipe for managing the nation's economy.[16] Churchill's cameo of the housewife, Mrs Kidd, who appeals to Marlene to forgo her promotion in favour of her overlooked husband, highlights the explosive collision between the patriarchal structures that condition women's role in the domestic sphere and women's masculinist masquerade in the workplace. When her housewifely defence of her husband as the archetypal male breadwinner with three children to support fails, Mrs Kidd denounces Marlene as 'one of these ballbreakers' (1990a: 113). 'Could you please piss off?' is Marlene's 'tough bird' response (1990a:113). This is a pivotal moment: a contestation of the image of woman as 'ballbreaker'*and* housewife that Thatcher personified. It reveals what the Thatcherite image-making conceals: the antagonistic divide between the patriarchally configured housewife and top-girl achiever; the two cannot be reconciled.

Furthermore, Thatcher's resurrection of a post-war-styled Patient Griselda fails to recognise the wage-less housewife who also works: to see the reality for a woman like Marlene's working-class sister, Joyce. With her four cleaning jobs and care of Marlene's daughter, Angie, Joyce is the sister who feels the loss of socialism as an egalitarian force for change. No adventures for Joyce; 'I'm right here where I was,' she says in the play's third act set in the kitchen of the sisters' childhood home (Churchill 1990a: 124). Staying put, she is bound to the generational cycles of wasted lives – 'nothing's changed for most people' (Churchill 1990a: 139), not least for women like Joyce, who would have benefited from a living wage and affordable childcare, if not *free* childcare as per the demand of second-wave feminism.[17] But both of these represent "poor"

---

[16] Thatcher's address of women as housewives dates back to her 1975 speeches. For details, see Campbell 1987: 234.

[17] State provision for twenty-four-hour nurseries was one of the four demands established at the first national conference of the Women's Liberation Movement, Ruskin College, Oxford, 1970. The other three demands were for equal pay, equal education and opportunity, and free contraception and abortion on demand.

housekeeping according to Thatcherite economics. As Campbell explained, there was to be no 'claim on the social purse: the devaluation of women's skills was seen as a function of the market and therefore immutable, and childcare was to remain the mother's problem and therefore a private problem' (1987: 201).

In Joyce's care, Angie is treated to a kind of tough love; their relationship is characterised by an emotional poverty born of their harsh circumstances. As R. Darren Gobert points out, critics 'have been slower' to acknowledge the 'suspect' aspects of Joyce's maternal role compared to observing the sacrifices she made in taking on Angie (2014: 5). Joyce both aggressively defends Angie, yet also marks her down as 'stupid, lazy and frightened' (Churchill 1990a: 140).[18] Hence, between them, the sisters have consigned Angie to a dead-end future: Joyce sees Angie's prospects as limited by a lack of opportunity; Marlene will not lend a helping hand to those who are 'stupid, lazy and frightened'. However, blame for the nightmare that is Angie's 'Frightening' future (Churchill 1990a: 141) does not lie with Marlene and Joyce as individuals, but rather with the lack of structural change that denies *all* women the right to adventures. In short, it is not enough for the exceptional woman to change her life; it is society that needs to change, and, as a revolutionary socialist feminism demonstrates, this requires the radical transformation of the patriarchally configured family and masculinist workplace.

With the retention of Brechtian elements – the doubling/tripling of roles, non-linear structure and the opening act that disturbs or alienates the more naturalistic scenes in the subsequent two acts – *Top Girls* elicits those 'what-if-if-only' feelings for lost futures, for the lives that could have been lived differently. What the future looks like from either side of the socialist-capitalist divide comes to the fore in Marlene and Joyce's heated, us-and-them dialectical debate that closes the final act. Marlene's vision of a 'stupendous' time ahead (Churchill 1990a: 137) hinges on Thatcher's adoption of monetarism, belief in the individual, demise of the 'slimy unions' (Churchill 1990a: 138) and abjection of the working class. No less vitriolic in her outpouring against capitalism, Joyce sees a 'stupendous' future rooted in working-class resistance to exploitation. There is a revolutionary note as Joyce declares 'we'll get you lot off our backs' (Churchill 1990a: 140) that echoes the account Dull Gret gives of her peasant women's revolt at the close of Act One. Except, the uprising Joyce forecasts is one problematically envisioned in the workers' movement embedded in the trade unions – problematic because of its patriarchal lineage as exemplified by the description of the sisters' father, a poor agricultural labourer

---

[18] See also Joyce in Act Two as she badmouths Angie and threatens to lock her out of the house when she will not come in from the yard (Churchill 1990a: 91).

who, while hostile to the 'Bosses still walking on the workers' faces' (Churchill 1990a: 138), was also the man who 'drank the money' (Churchill 1990a: 139) and hit his wife. Thus, the working-class woman stands alone: she is unsupported by an unreconstructed, soon-to-be-decimated labour movement[19] *and* a feminism losing its collective, socialist outlook to its right-wing, top-girl double.

Although theatre critics were initially lukewarm when *Top Girls* first opened,[20] over the decades it has come to be widely regarded as a seminal, state-of-the-nation play in British theatre – a drama that probes the country's enduring socio-economic, class-based, 'us' and 'them' divide despite successive governments vaunting the idea of a classless society. In 2019 when the Royal National Theatre revived *Top Girls,* Jessie Thompson from the *Evening Standard* published a series of reflections from actresses who had performed in different productions of the play. In this collectively voiced piece, what emerges is the overriding view that 'in a changing world' so extraordinarily little has changed for women. As Lesley Sharp (Dull Gret/Angie; Royal Court revival, 1991) reflects: 'Have things changed? Have they really changed? It's astounding that *Top Girls* in each of its several incarnations since the original production has felt that the question is fresh minted and the answers are still mired in ambivalence' (qtd in Thompson 2019). Other comments also refer to the theatre industry's persistent inequalities, thereby attesting to the enduring importance of *Top Girls* as a rare example of an all-female play that is formally inventive and politically prescient in its original and subsequent 'incarnations'.

Like her production of *Light Shining in Buckinghamshire*, director Lyndsey Turner's 2019 revival of *Top Girls* at the National also had a large cast. This I experienced as detrimental to the political significances that derive from the convention of doubling (e.g. the doubling of Dull Gret and Angie that underscores their "bottom" girl status), but advantageous to the agency scenes: as multiple women traversed the office space, so they heightened the sense of strenuous, achieving-related activity. More interesting from the point of view of casting and the play's political dynamics was the production directed by Suba Das at Liverpool's Everyman Theatre in 2023. With Churchill's blessing, Das opted for an inclusive and diverse cast.[21] It was the first major UK production to cast a Black woman in the role of Marlene (Tala Gouveia). The casting of

---

[19] Thatcher's defeat of the Miners' strike (1984–5) heralded the catastrophic dismantling of the Trade Unions' power to negotiate on behalf of workers.
[20] For comments on the reception of *Top Girls*, see Little and McLaughlin 2007: 232.
[21] Das' consultations with Churchill with regard to the casting were explained at 'Caryl Churchill and feminist theatre: A roundtable discussion hosted by the University of Liverpool', 18 March 2023.

ethnically diverse women combined with relocating the childhood home of the sisters from its original East Anglian setting to Liverpool's Toxteth (the site of racially-ignited, inner-city rioting in 1981) brought a race-related dynamic to Churchill's socialist interrogation of feminism. On the one hand, a sense of ethnicity as a barrier to women's success pervaded the agency scenes in which Marlene/Gouveia appeared as the only Black presence. On the other hand, the racial dimension also reinvigorated Churchill's critique of Thatcherite individualism: this will not serve to create a more socially progressive future for the Toxteth, working-class, Black family and community Marlene has left behind.

2.2 An Eco-Socialist-Feminist Aesthetic: *Fen*

There is an energy to *Top Girls* that derives from Churchill's dramatisation of the desire to achieve, and the verve of the overlapping dialogue is replete with lines that are by turns barbed and comedic, thereby rendering a tonal mix of the dark and the light. *Fen*, that Churchill began working on after the opening of *Top Girls*, is altogether darker. Composed of twenty-one scenes designed to be played continuously, each with an attitudinally formed social purpose, the play is Brechtian in form, though also poetically spartan, moving from one short scenic episode to another, always in the same setting. Its content drew on a Joint Stock workshop conducted in the Fens; the inclusion of things that were told to the company by the villagers they met in the Fenlands, made it the 'most documentary' of Churchill's works at that time (BBC: 1988). And with a cast of five women and one man playing twenty-two parts, Churchill again made women central to her theatrical landscape as she embarked on her socialist interrogation of agrarian-based exploitation.

The motif of a woman wanting to change her life also reappears: Val, a married, poorly remunerated labourer, attempts to leave the Fens for London, where she imagines starting a new life with her two, young daughters and lover, Frank. But like all the other Fenland women, she is economically constrained by the rural environment and a moral, "Christian" code that forbids her seeking happiness outside of the marital home. The thwarted love affair between Val and Frank is the catalyst for the play's action, but this story-line is threaded through a much larger social canvas that recounts stories of oppression, past and present. Hence, Churchill elicits a mode of engagement that hinges on what Juliet Mitchell describes as a process of 'identifying' as distinct from 'identifying with' (2021: 1037). To elaborate: Mitchell makes this important distinction when analysing the fiction of Raymond Williams and the way he invites readers to 'accompany him on a learning journey about past and present and possible future' histories of the subjects he writes about (2021). Not then a 'narrative' but a 'learning journey' (2021). Similarly, the 'learning journey' Churchill and members of the Joint Stock company undertook when they researched the Fenland community is one that she invites us to accompany her on in *Fen*. To learn about the lives she dramatises is to 'identify' how they are shaped as they are, rather than to be caught up in 'identifying with' a narrative tale of failed romance.

A sense of 'identifying' also underpins Churchill's political perspective: her portrait of the Fenland community identifies and impresses the need for the Left to re-think its socialist agenda. There are various ways in which Churchill posits a 'learning journey' for the renewal of socialism that, as the ensuing discussion will demonstrate, include recognition of: the exploited female labourer/homeworker; an ecologically aware approach to the management of natural resources; the unions as an historically male preserve; and the global forces of capitalism and their impact on labour relations.

In *Fen*, according to the farmer Tewson, the women who labour in the fields picking potatoes are 'Better workers than men' (Churchill 1990a: 171). What he 'admires' is their capacity to keep on working in his 'fields with icicles on their faces' (1990a: 171). But there is little to admire about the cross-generations of women being forced to labour in these extreme weather conditions – forced, because if they do not work, they do not get paid. As established in Scene 2, they are a cheap labour force overseen by a female gangmaster, a woman with 'two colour tellies to spoil' (1990a: 149) and largely devoid of affective caregiving to those women who work for her. Imaging women in their hunched-over, backbreaking lines of repetitive potato-picking as representative of the working class, displaces the iconic image of industrial man on the factory-based assembly line. With regard to the latter, Hall explained, 'that sort of labour regime' was diminishing, and this 'older socialist imagery [was] collapsing' (1988: 245). In one way, Churchill's woman-centred re-imaging of the proletariat gestures to the Left's need to expand its gender-blind horizon. In another, its agrarian rather than industrial imagery posits an ecological dimension to the 'labour regime' with which the Left needs to align. In brief, the Left's 'learning journey' towards renewal involves recognition of capitalism's exploitation of women's labour *and* the land.

In the 1980s, progress on the Left was hindered by the way in which 'many people' were 'still in the age of "Before Planet Earth" – i.e., before the ecological consciousness of the finite character of global resources dawned' (Hall 1988: 249). The need for an eco-socialist awareness and approach to natural resources comes to the fore in *Fen* as Churchill identifies how histories of capitalist commodification of the land have failed to prioritise people's needs and welfare over profit. The play opens with a Japanese businessman alluding to the seventeenth-century 'rich lords' who 'planned to drain fen' – a plan that met with resistance from the Fen dwellers who wanted 'to keep fish and eels to live on' (1990a: 147).[22] As Mary Chamberlain in *Fenwomen* – one of Churchill's resources – elaborates: 'Reclaimed land was given as payment to the men who carried out the drainage, not to the men from whom the land had been taken' (1977: 14). Resistance was fierce, 'many fen legends tell of the triumph of the fen "Tigers" – as they were nicknamed – in sabotaging the system', and yet the drainage project prevailed (1977: 14).

Historically, the 'East Anglian landworkers were in the vanguard of the battle for unionisation' (1977: 15). In the play, there is talk of the unions. The ninety-year-old Ivy (Val's grandmother) recollects the workers being too afraid of 'old Tewson' to sign up, although they did refuse the farmer's overtures to vote Tory: '"Vote for the blues, boys," he'd say and he'd give them money to drink. They'd pull off the blue ribbons behind the hedge. Still have the drink though' (Churchill 1990a: 177–178). This historical detail links to the present: in Scene 3, Frank, *'talking to himself'* (Churchill 1990a: 150), imagines having a conversation with the present-day Tewson in which the idea that he might join the union in the interests of securing a better wage is rejected; of Tewson guilt-tripping Frank into accepting poor remuneration for his labour by citing the benefits in kind the farmer has bestowed on him and his father before him. This two-way conversation voiced by Frank concludes in an action that signals their non-unionised arrangement as an act of self-harm: 'Frank *hits* Mr TEWSON, *that is he hits himself across the face*' (Churchill 1990a: 151). The Brechtian feeling structure of this gestic action invites us to feel-see not the individual's pain, but the harm caused by an unjust, exploitative system of low-waged production. Moreover, the schizophrenic split between power and powerlessness enacted in the self-same body in this scene is maintained throughout: the roles of Frank and Tewson are doubled.

However, as noted in the discussion of *Top Girls*, the unions are a male preserve. The working-class struggle against exploitation, rooted in the "soil" of socialism, excludes women's double exploitation on the land and in the home. In the fields the women work by hand (not with machinery) – mind-numbing, repetitive labour, after which there is still the domestic labour to complete. In Scene 11, the fifty-year-old labourer Shirley is seen relentlessly moving *'from one job to another, ironing, mending, preparing dinner, minding a baby'*. She *'never stops throughout the scene'* (Churchill 1990a: 167). As the actress Jennie Stoller (Val) recollects, in the workshopping process all cast members under

---

[22] Resistance to the drainage of the Fenlands is also cited in *Light Shining in Buckinghamshire*; Churchill 1985: 225.

took an 'exercise [that] involved completing a set of [domestic] physical tasks in a limited space of time' – a way of sensing the experience of the Fenland women who 'seemed to do everything – work in the field, organise the home, bring up the children' (qtd in Roberts 2008: 221). Ultimately, their 'learning journey' in the Fens left them with a lasting impression of the women's dual labour; it was 'their experience that had left its mark on us all' (qtd in Roberts 2008: 221).

The director Peter Brook once reflected on whether theatre had a capacity to leave its 'mark'. In the case of a 'striking theatrical experience', he claimed that it is 'the play's central image that remains' – a 'kernel engraved' on a spectator's 'memory' (1972: 152). The 'central image' that lingers in my memory of *Fen* is of the mist-laden field that "houses" the women's domestic and agricultural labour (designed by Annie Smart). Imaging a group of working-class women in a field that is also a room (a cooker or a chair "planted" in the soil) rendered an eco-socialist-feminist aesthetic – the 'kernel' of the play's ecologically aware, socialist-feminist dynamics.

The field/room was recreated in *The Caryl Churchill Omnibus*; four of the original cast members played extracts from Scenes 6 and 9, juxtaposing the domestic cruelty of the former with the histories of Fenland violence in the latter. 'My stepmother used to make me drink boiling hot tea' is the recorded note from Churchill's Fenland research that cues Scene 6 (BBC: 1988). The violence Angela (Amelda Brown) inflicts on her step-daughter is quick and calculated as she pivots from the stove to face Becky (Tricia Kelly), her arm extended, her hand holding out the mug of boiling hot liquid. A defiant but tearful Becky is ultimately defeated. She would like to be a hairdresser; her if-only yearnings for a different kind of job are chorused in the 'Girls' Song' that closes Scene 7. But as the image of the cooker in the soil reminds us, her future is bound to the land and domesticity just as it is for all the generations of the Fenland women, past and present. There is no escape; akin to Angie in *Top Girls*, the only outlet Becky has is her secret notebook.

An angry letter written to a farmer at the time of the Littleport Riots (1816; Churchill 1990a: ix) when extreme poverty saw Fenlanders take to the roads demanding bread, is the source for Churchill's ghost of the woman whose 'baby died starving' (Churchill 1990a: 163). In the filmed extract from Scene 9, Jennie Stoller as the ghost (the role doubles with Val) appears to Tewson (Bernard Strother); she is first seen crouched down in the potato field – a haunting reprise of the contemporary women's backs bent to make a profit for the bosses. Her body gradually unfolds, becoming upright, as she holds Tewson/Strother in her angry gaze, moving confrontationally towards him, while delivering the speech that rails against the farmers who made a living off the poor. Like an ancient Greek Fury, she seeks vengeance for a system that still does not change.

Things are changing in one way, although not to the benefit of the labourers. High taxation of the land is forcing farmers like Tewson to sell-out to big companies. Owners whose lands have been passed down through the generations now find themselves tenants; the father-to-son system of inheritance is no longer secure (an echo of butcher Clegg's failed dynasty in *Owners*). International businesses own the English soil of the Fenlands. As the *Japanese* businessman proclaims, 'Esso, Gallagher, Imperial Tobacco, Equitable Life, all love this excellent earth' (Churchill 1990a: 147). Hall observed that with the advent of this kind of globalised capitalism, socialism would have to contend with the accelerated 'drive towards privatization' and the 'new international division of labour' (1988: 246). Globally owned, private businesses erode the clear demarcation between bosses and workers, the divide that historically marked the unions' battle line for strike action. As Nell, the non-conformist troublemaker, asks: 'So who's boss? Who do you have a go at? Acton's was Ross, Ross is Imperial Foods, Imperial Foods is Imperial Tobacco, so where does that stop?' (Churchill 1990a: 181).

Seeing no end to a lifecycle of misery, Val invites Frank to kill her with an axe.[23] Defying the logic of mortality, the murdered Val reappears and unleashes a liminal space which, akin to *What If If Only's* spirit-inhabited zone, is haunted by the ghosts of lost futures. A resistant yearning ruptures the play's final imaging of the Fenland women: a stilt-walking Nell proclaims she 'won't turn back'; Shirley irons the field and recounts the poor from the past killing farm animals to release their anger; and May, who can't sing, sings (1990a: 189). Pain is palpable as Becky is seen trapped in the nightmare of abuse, taunted by Angela, who hurts her because she herself is hurting, and there are so many dead children clamouring to be heard. Val focuses on the tale of a girl whose if-only request to 'see spring again' was granted by the Fens' boggarts (malevolent spirits) on the understanding that she would not 'live longer than one of the cowslips at the gate' (1990a: 188). Spring proves restorative, but when a boy 'picks a cowslip without much noticing', the girl turns into 'a wrinkled white dead thing like the cowslip' (1990a: 188). There is an eco-radical-feminist resonance to the image of the boy who thoughtlessly crushes the life out of the girl and nature – a closing, salutary reminder that *man*kind is 'still in the age of "Before Planet Earth"' and still in the age of patriarchy.However, overall, it is an eco-*socialist*-feminism that reverberates throughout *Fen* with its imaging of working-class women bound to the earth that is privately, globally owned. The play has not had a history of revivals comparable to *Top Girls* and is deserving

---

[23] The killing is prefigured in the tale Nell tells about lovers murdered by an avenging husband; Scene 10.

of more re-stagings[24] on account of its finely rendered feeling structures that impress the need for an eco-egalitarian future that is still not yet. And as this side-by-side re-viewing of the two plays hopefully attests, the case for an eco-aware-feminist socialism that *Fen* evinces is as critical as the case *Top Girls* makes for a socialist feminism. Both are necessary for the Left's long 'hard road to renewal'.

2.3 Anti-Capitalist Critique and the Shapeshifting Skriker

Rahel Jaeggi writing with Nancy Fraser observes that in critical theory 'sometime in the mid- to late 1980s', capitalism 'pretty much dropped out of the picture' (Fraser & Jaeggi 2023: 3). Elsewhere, referring to this period, Fraser more specifically cites capitalism as 'all but vanished from the agenda of *feminist* theory' (2013: 227; emphasis added). Distancing themselves 'from the sort of large-scale social theorizing associated with Marxism', feminist theorists eschewed critical attentions to capitalism as 'reductive, deterministic and dépassé' (2013: 227). By contrast, Churchill the socialist-feminist theatre maker increasingly moved capitalism centre stage, inviting her audiences to feel-think the damaging consequences of an exploitative economic system. The critique of global capitalism that surfaced in *Fen* is renewed later in the decade with *Serious Money*. Opening at the Royal Court in March 1987, shortly before Thatcher's landslide re-election, the play was a high-octane, satirical take on London's international money markets with its new breed of young, working-class male marketeers clashing with gentrified, old-guard bankers, and high-flying women devoted to material greed (Marlene would have been proud). It was another Joint Stock production; the company's ensemble "traded" in a rhythmically versed language of the markets (helpfully, as I recall, explained in the programme notes). At the close, the cast were left chorusing 'Five More Glorious Years' of Thatcherism (Churchill 1990a: 308); not all audiences grasped the satirical note (see Aston 2010: 74). However, in the remaining space of this Section, it is the Thatcherite legacy of global capitalism as an ecologically damaging force that I want to bring fully into focus by turning to Churchill's mid-1990s play, *The Skriker*. Where *Fen* ends in the death zone with its folktale of the young girl 'a wrinkled white dead thing like the cowslip', so *The Skriker* begins – enters the folkloric, spirit underworld that haunts and distorts the world as we know it.

The Skriker premiered in January 1994 at the National, rather than Churchill's usual Royal Court home. Thatcher was out (forced to resign in

---

[24] For details of *Fen's* 'first London revival' at the Finborough Theatre in 2011, see Gobert 2014: 150–151.

1990), but the 'Glorious Years' of Conservatism (note the ironic tone) were not yet over: Prime Minister John Major held the reins of a Tory government still enthralled to free-market capitalism, a creed of individualism, and reduction in state welfare. Major's 'overriding concern' was, as Phil Burton-Cartledge summarised, to make the 'Thatcherite counterrevolution permanent' (2021: 97). A Labour government was still some three years away, though as Section 3 will elaborate, the advent of Tony Blair's *New* Labour government in 1997 did not auger socialism's renewal. Moreover, a 'new feminism' was vaunting a Marlene-styled revival of female empowerment, reclaiming Thatcher as 'the great unsung heroine of British feminism' (Walter 1999: 175). In brief, 'The Great Moving Right Show' premiered by Thatcher was still playing as Churchill's mythological creature, the Skriker, took to the stage.

The production – a collaboration with the Second Stride dance-theatre company – was another 'striking theatrical experience':[25] dancers playing the Skriker's underworld spirits rendered movement-based, feeling structures of an ecologically damaged realm, the responsibility for which rests with humankind. The memorable image – the 'kernel' that Brook advised might serve to 'reconstruct a set of meanings' – was Kathryn Hunter's shapeshifting Skriker. The image of the Skriker/Hunter at the start of the performance, with her moth-like wings and spidery, contorted limbs in hues of black and grey, is the 'kernel' out of which the meaning of the play unfolds. In her opening monologue in which her fairytale language is as deformed as her twisted limbs, this ancient fairy 'speaks bitterness' against the human race that hate her spirit kind. Malevolent, like the boggarts in the Fenland marshes, the Skriker appears to us as a ghostly, ghastly creature seeking vengeance for the 'rivers of blood poisoning' the earth (Churchill 1994: 4).[26] Poised for flight at the close of the monologue, she is set to enact and unleash her cautionary tale of planetary destruction on a world where the global forces of 'serious money' exploit natural resources and birth a still-born future.

Two young mothers are the only mortal remains on earth as we know it; one has already killed her baby (Josie); the other is pregnant (Lily). Both are preyed on by the Skriker, who has designs on Lily's baby. On the one hand, the Skriker controls and manipulates the young women with her ancient, fairy magic. On the other hand, starved of human affection, she is a needy creature, one who seeks kindness in the guise of an old woman begging the 'price of a cup of tea' (Churchill 1994: 11) or a child wanting maternal comfort. As the ensuing

---

[25] This is my own, personal view; a majority of theatre critics were either baffled or critical, if not both.
[26] The theme of toxicity resonant in *The Skriker* had been explored in Churchill's previous collaboration with Second Stride: *The Lives of the Poisoners* (1991).

discussion will elucidate, through the encounters she stages between Josie, Lily and the Skriker, Churchill bridges worlds of social and ecological damage to render a dystopian outlook for the century's end.

No less concerned about a socialist renewal of the Left than Hall (or, for that matter, Churchill), Raymond Williams in *Towards 2000* expressed his anxiety that there was a danger of 'weakening or forgetting' that, unlike socialism, 'the capitalist system is against the general interest' (1983: 163). 'What makes this worse', he elaborated, 'is that the forms in which we have been offered the general interest [...] are demonstrably false': they disguise the reality of 'a systematically and radically unequal society' and a 'privileged and exploiting financial and economic order' (1983: 165). How to render that 'false' representation of 'the general interest' in ways that leave a 'mark' is a constant challenge for Churchill as it is for all artists committed to social change. In *The Skriker*, she disturbs social realism's familiar trope of working-class-girls-in-trouble:[27] locating Lily and Josie in the '*mental health hospital*' (Churchill 1994: 5) where the latter is incarcerated, the girls are propelled into the surreal, "deranged" world of the Skriker; a Kelpie spirit is already in attendance. The two worlds are fused; both are damaged. Like the Skriker, they 'don't work properly' (Churchill 1994: 48). This politicised linkage persists throughout the play, not least because, like the girls, the Skriker is an abject being: she is classed as a minor spirit – '*one of the many*, not a major spirit' (Churchill 1994: 16; emphasis added). Hence Churchill bridges a socialist-feminist concern for a class of "worthless" young mothers[28] with an ecological critique of the capitalist forces whose domination of the *under*world (nature) portends planetary destruction.

The Skriker struggles to remember an age when 'the general interest' extended to her spirit kind – a time when 'people knew we mattered' (Churchill 1994: 16). Parasitically feeding off human lives, she has learnt to imitate human ways. What the Skriker has discovered is that the human 'heart's desire' (Churchill 1994: 22) is for a 'taste waste of money', the 'buckets of bloodmoney' (Churchill 1994: 12). Imitating the human 'them' who 'hate us and hurtle faster and master' (Churchill 1994: 4), she emulates their 'bloodmoney' ways. In the guise of a '*smart WOMAN in mid thirties*' the Skriker reports on her 'fame and fortune telling' and 'market farces' (Churchill 1994: 36); businessmen with Thrumpins[29] on their backs prefigure the announcement

---

[27] Plays from the 1980s by the regrettably short-lived, working-class playwright Angela Dunbar exemplify this tradition, notably her high-profile *Rita Sue and Bob Too* (Royal Court, 1982).

[28] On the demonisation of lone mothers current at the time, see my observations in Aston 2003: 32.

[29] A Thrumpin is a 'kind of attendant demon, believed to haunt every man with the power of taking his life' (Royal National Theatre 1994: n.p.).

of her success. This is the disguise that unmasks what ecofeminist Val Plumwood termed the 'devouring', 'totalising self': the 'master identity' concealed within the 'global Rational Economy' that consumes natural resources and colonises all life forms within the 'empire of the self' (1993: 193).[30] 'Revengeance is gold mine', the Skriker announces in her opening monologue (Churchill 1994: 5); mining the 'market farces' she apes humans at their own self-serving, capitalist 'devouring' game. She will be the one 'to witness unprecedented catastrophe' (Churchill 1994: 44), since the human race will wreck its own self-destruction as it exploits and destroys the very means of its survival. As the Skriker observes, the humans she feeds off are no longer 'succulent' but 'Dry as dustpans' (Churchill 1994: 32).

Ultimately, it is her underworld that the Skriker wants to nourish and protect from the colonising master. Her initial attachment to baby-killer Josie, who might be goaded into wishing her dead baby back to breed/breathe new life into the underworld, lessens in favour of Lily, the good girl. Kindness is rewarded with fairy magic (Lily speaks coins; Churchill 1994: 11); nastiness is punished (Josie speaks toads; Churchill 1994: 19). And yet, paralleling the way in which Josie attempts to protect Lily from the lure of fairy magic by 'trying to keep the Skriker sated seated besotted with gobbets' (Churchill 1994: 49), Lily cannot save the natural world that the spirit realm represents. As Plumwood points out, the 'argument that it is the goodness of women that will save us', as posited in some versions of ecofeminism, will not suffice (1993: 9). Churchill underscores this point through the journeys each of the girls makes to the underworld. First Josie, lured to the spirit realm and succumbing to its 'glamour' that is nothing but a banquet of 'twigs and beetles and a dead body' (Churchill 1994: 30), is tricked into living years in the underworld which, when she manages to escape, constitutes a millisecond of time, thus allowing her to return to life as she left it. When Lily repeats Josie's journey in the belief that she will have the same time-travelling experience, she lands not in the spirit realm but an apocalyptic 'real world' (Churchill 1994: 51) – 'another cemetery, a black whole hundred yearns' (Churchill 1994: 52). There she is confronted by her female descendants, the youngest of whom '*bellows wordless rage*' on discovery that her ancestor hailed from 'the distant past master class' (Churchill 1994: 51). In brief, in ecological terms, time is running out to reverse the 'devouring' trend of global-capitalist forces.

Such a reversal majorly depends, as Churchill demonstrated in *Light Shining in Buckinghamshire* and *Fen*, on land being publicly, commonly owned and

---

[30] The global reproduction of the 'empire of the self' same is also alluded to in the play as Lily attempts to explain how televised images are beamed around the world so that the Skriker can understand how it is possible 'to see all over the world' (Churchill 1994: 13).

harvested to nourish people not plenish profit. In *The Skriker*, the need to steer a different course in 'the general interest' is rendered palpable through the play's depiction of social inequalities in the 'real world', as represented by Josie and Lily, doubling with the hierarchical divide evinced between human and non-human species. If time is running out, then so too is the space for non-human life forms. The spirits lack a liveable space of their own; like the vengeful ghost of the Fenlands, they haunt the human world. As Plumwood observes, the 'living things, beings who move to their own rhythms' and not to the tune of the master race are 'denied space and place' (1993: 193). In the National's production, Annie Smart's clinically designed space with its cube-like inset housed both humans and spirits; motifs seeped from one species to the other (e.g. Lily's shoe transformed into a gigantic, fairytale replica; Churchill 1994: 41). Shadows on walls and marks on the white flooring disturbed the idea of a pristine order; 'otherness' imprinted the space as the dancer-spirits 'moved to their own rhythms'. This double-eyed aesthetic that blends the two worlds together invites us to see what the one-eyed human race overlooks.[31] Hence, Churchill's admonition that in the interests of an ecologically sustainable future we must learn to recognise and radically transform our hierarchical human/non-human relations. Otherwise, what awaits is Lily's 'horror storybook ending' (Churchill 1994: 52).

Over the years, I found it hard to imagine any other performer in the role of the Skriker; Hunter made the part so completely her own. As the play's director Les Waters commented, 'The Skriker is one of the great roles written for women. Kathryn Hunter played it with her characteristic brilliance. I think we would have been fucked if she'd not been available, or turned down the role' (qtd in Roberts 2008: 248). However, the consummate actress and socialist activist Maxine Peake proved the exception. The play was revived in 2015 at the Royal Exchange Theatre Manchester in a production directed by Sarah Frankcom.[32] As I blogged at the time, Peake 'captivated and enthralled as she adopted one disguise after another' (Aston 2015). The banquet scene presided over by Peake's raggedy-regal, Elizabethan-styled Skriker-queen, 'was devastatingly, brutally exquisite in its rendition of the spirits feasting on one their own'; the 'asylum-styled setting' designed by Lizzie Clachan rendered 'a heightened sense of the insanity of self-serving greed' (Aston 2015).

---

[31] Note that the spirits are visible to the audience, but are unseen by Josie and Lily. The Skriker becomes visible to the girls when in *human* form.

[32] Peake also reprised the role of the Skriker in a radio adaptation of the play broadcast on BBC Radio 3, 20 March 2016. The adaptation pared back the roles to just those of the Skriker, Josie and Lily. Sarah Frankcom again directed.

As this 2015 revival of *The Skriker* attests, 'the insanity of self-serving greed' purportedly in 'the 'general interest' of the nation did not desist. With the forces of global capitalism strengthening and the Skriker's ecological clock still ticking, Section 3 explores Churchill's structures of world-ending, dystopian feeling.

3 The Political is Personal

When *What If If Only*'s Someone attempts to summon up his dead loved one, 'the ghost of a future that never happened' who comes in their stead explains that: 'if you can make me happen then there would be your beloved real person not a ghost your real real living because what happened will never have happened' (Churchill 2021: 9). Thus, Someone's personal loss of their 'beloved' is inextricably linked to the political: a world in which the loved one survives rather than dies is one in which the alternative 'future that never happened' happens. The ghost insists change is possible, but it is up to the 'living' to 'make things happen'. 'Don't let me go', the spirit pleads (Churchill 2021: 9).

However, as Section 2 demonstrated, around the turn of the millennium Churchill's vision for an ecologically aware, egalitarian future forged in socialist-feminist values was in danger of being let go, was threatened with extinction. Neoliberalism's hegemonic hold, inaugurated by Margaret Thatcher and sustained by successive governments, perpetuated the idea that there was no alternative to neoliberal, free-market capitalism, now operating on a global scale. As analysis of *Far Away* in this Section will reveal, Churchill's strategy was to posit a reverse formulation by depicting how an anti-democratic regime enmeshed in the global forces of capitalism threatens world extinction in a Hobbesian-styled 'war of all against all'.[33] Moreover, as the title of this third Section indicates, there is another reversal under consideration: the shift from the second-wave feminist mantra 'the personal is political' to the 'political is personal'. This signals Churchill's attention to the negative emotional impact that an anti-democratic regime has on people's every day, personal lives. The political is personal is explored in relation to *Far Away* and its depiction of a totalitarian state; it surfaces again in my discussion of her more recent play, *Escaped Alone* (2016) in which political voicings of planetary annihilation haunt the personal lives of four older women. Drawing on Hannah Proctor's *Burnout: The Emotional Experience of*

---

[33] I refer here to the famous phrase, 'a war of all against all', by the philosopher Thomas Hobbes who lived through the turbulent times of the English civil war that Churchill depicts in *Light Shining in Buckinghamshire*.

Political Defeat (2024), analysis of *Escaped Alone* also explores the issue of personal well-being in times of political activism and 'defeat'.

The feeling structures of these two plays are radically different to the Brechtian conventions and techniques that were seminal to the double-eyed vision of her former work (as detailed in Sections 1 and 2): both evince her twenty-first-century turn to a condensed, and poetic mode of theatre. To reflect on the significance of this formal shift in Churchill's playwriting, in conjunction with offering preliminary reflections on relations between the political and the personal at the turn of the century and the advent of New Labour, I refer first to her 1997, short play, *This is a Chair*.

3.1 A Political and Personal Disconnect: *This Is a Chair*

In the years preceding the election of his New Labour government on 1 May 1997, Tony Blair undertook a radical transformation of the Labour Party. As trade unionist Andrew Murray elucidates, by disarticulating the Party's historical links to socialism, Blair was 'essentially remaking it as a post-socialist, post-class and even to an extent post-democratic party' (2019: 67).[34] There would be no reversal of the neoliberal, free-market economy, but rather the party's 'explicit reconciliation with the new unbounded capitalism sweeping the world' (2019: 66). In short, with the Left moving towards or even morphing into the Right, the neoliberal hegemony remained unchallenged with only the remnants of a marginalised, socialist left committed to the 'hard road to renewal'. Thus, feeling the loss of a socialist vision was symptomatic of New Labour times.

Equally, displaced by its neoliberal, 'top-girl' double, a socially progressive feminism was at risk of becoming an endangered species: a conservative media rebranded feminism as girl power. 'Pulled in the direction of the political right', girl power endorsed 'brutal individualism and the pursuit of wealth and success', thereby transforming 'personal and social relationships into an extension of the market economy' (McRobbie 2000: 211).

With regard to ecological matters, the priority given to free-market economics meant that natural resources were still being "harvested" in the interests of capitalist profit. Reflecting on 'third way' politics, theorised by Anthony Giddens and adopted by Blair, Chantal Mouffe posited that so 'many of the problems related to the environment have to do with neo-liberal policies' and 'their prioratizing [*sic*] of profit and market mechanisms' (2005: 17).

---

[34] The rewriting of Clause Four of the Labour Party's constitution – the clause that pledged a socialist commitment to workers' rights – signalled Blair's disarticulation of socialism. Although previous Labour governments by no means fully endorsed the original socialist spirit of the clause, none were as dismissive as New Labour. For details see Murray 2019: 67–69.

Immediately after New Labour's election, Churchill announced 'The Labour Party's Slide to the Right' in *This is a Chair*, staged by the Royal Court Theatre at the Duke of York's Theatre, London (June 1997).[35] Churchill selected this title for one of the play's eight scenes. She assigned each scene a title referring to a significant social or political issue, with the instruction that each title had to 'be clearly displayed or announced' (Churchill 2008: 40). However, the accompanying scenes bear no relation to the announcements. For instance, the scene entitled 'The Labour Party's Slide to the Right' (Churchill 2008: 45) depicts a distraught woman whose boyfriend has jumped off the balcony of their third-floor apartment, seemingly after being confronted and threatened by her two brothers who accused him of getting their sister addicted to drugs. Nothing is clarified, developed or concluded. The action is suspended; suffused with a sense of menace and violence, the scenic fragment is simply left hanging. The same obtains for all other scenes: a dramatic situation is glimpsed but abandoned in favour of another.

The disconnect between the announcement of political topics and dramatic vignettes dismantles the Brechtian convention of titling episodic scenes with a socially orientated purpose, as exemplified by *Light Shining in Buckinghamshire*. Instead, the estrangement between the two signals an abject failure to connect to the bigger, political picture – registers a divorce between the political and the personal. Individuals are caught up in the trivia of everyday life (the opening scene titled 'The War in Bosnia' depicts a couple on a London street having to re-arrange a time to meet up); personal quarrels (a gay lovers' tiff accompanies the fifth 'Hong Kong' scene); or dramatic events, as in the scene captioned by 'The Labour Party's Swing to the Right'. Not even the possibility that a bomb might have exploded is enough to disturb a couple from retiring to bed in the play's penultimate scene. It was probably the noise of building work, or maybe even a firework going off, is how the couple allay their fears and retreat into the rhythms of their domestic, walled-in existence.

This sequence of dramatic fragments fosters an overriding sense of theatre in existential crisis – a crisis over the meaning and purpose of theatre that was heightened in the original production by reconfiguring the spatial arrangement between performers and spectators. With the audience relocated to the stage and the actors situated 'on a platform spread across the centre stalls' (Roberts 2008: 137), the performance prompted questions about performer–spectator relations, about the dynamics between what happens on stage and in the auditorium.

---

[35] This West End venue provided a temporary home for the Royal Court company while their Sloane Square premises underwent major, lottery-funded refurbishment. *This is a Chair* was staged twice daily for just four nights (25–28 June 1997) with a cast of luminaries from the London International Festival of Theatre.

Marion Bailey, who played the mother in a menacing, patriarchally controlled family dinner scene that is performed not once but twice at different times,[36] commented: 'somewhere along the line [Churchill] was asking a question of the audience. What was the territory she should be exploring as a playwright of the nineties? And what is the nature of the theatre' (qtd in Roberts 2008: 252).

If Churchill had designed a caption to announce *This is a Chair* it might have been worded 'This is Not a Play', akin to Magritte's famous painting The Treachery of Images, otherwise known as This is Not a Pipe, that was chosen to illustrate the cover of the play's initial publication in 1999.[37] As Churchill explains, *This is a Chair* and other works staged in 1997 – *Hotel* performed by Second Stride, and *Blue Heart* staged by Out of Joint and the Royal Court Theatre – all come from a 'similar mindset': that of undermining the notion of a play that each purports to be (2008: vii). '*Hotel* isn't a play but an opera libretto' (2008: vii); it is actually formed of two pieces themed on urban alienation that could, Churchill advises, be performed separately. Similarly, the absurdly conceived *Blue Heart* is a duo of plays: '*Heart's Desire* is a play that can't happen, obsessively resetting itself back to the beginning every time it veers off-course. *Blue Kettle* is a play infected with a virus' (2008: vii).

All of this work evinces Churchill writing towards a more experimental, condensed, elliptical mode of theatre. Specific to *This is a Chair* is her experimentation with what form politically committed theatre can take at a time of depoliticisation that is detrimental to our capacity to connect to the bigger political picture, nationally and globally. The Brechtian signature of political theatre will no longer serve as the repeated undermining of the titles reflects. And note too that when the play ends, it concludes with a scene that has no content, only a title: 'The Impact of Capitalism on the Former Soviet Union' (Churchill 2008: 58). The title juxtaposed with an empty stage/blank page ultimately confirms the cancellation of this mode of political theatre-making.

3.2 *Far Away* and the Turn to the Political Is Personal

Churchill's reference to the former Soviet Union in *This Is a Chair*'s final, unaccompanied title, is a reminder of the historic, early 1990s collapse of communism in the USSR and other countries in the Eastern Bloc – a collapse that fuelled the political right's discrediting of socialism as a worthy opponent to capitalism. With that breakdown came what Mouffe analyses as 'a largely unipolar world', the political impact of which, she argues, is the suppression

---

[36] Only the titles change from 'Pornography and Censorship' to 'The Northern Ireland Peace Process'. Hence, the patriarchal authority depicted in the vignette remains and repeats.

[37] For an analysis of a Magritte influence on the aesthetics of the play and a fuller discussion of *This is a Chair* than I have space for here, see Aston 2013.

of 'alternatives to the dominant [neoliberal] hegemonic order' (2013: 19). With regard to international relations, she critiques millennial strains of consensus-based cosmopolitan democracy, arguing that the wholesale adoption if not imposition of a 'Western model', 'eliminates the possibility of legitimate dissent, thereby creating a favourable terrain for the emergence of violent forms of antagonisms' (2013: 20).[38]

The 'violent forms of antagonisms' posed by a unipolar world dictated by a Western mode of capitalising natural resources comes to the fore in the apocalyptic landscape of *Far Away*, premiered at the Royal Court Theatre in 2000. Moving beyond or breaking through the 'mindset' of writing plays that self-destruct, this ecological drama 'isn't being undermined' (Churchill 2008: viii). The play is compressed and elliptical; it features just three characters – Joan, her Aunt Harper and her boyfriend, Todd. But the three, elliptically styled parts that make up *Far Away* do connect up through the figure of Joan who is first seen as a child in the home of her Aunt Harper, then as an adult making hats to be worn by condemned prisoners paraded before execution, and finally as a soldier in a war of all against all. Together, this trio of scenes registers the loss of feminist, socialist, and ecological feeling: the girl child inherits a frightening future (the ghosts of Angie in *Top Girls* or Becky in *Fen* are not 'far away'); exploitive labour relations under capitalism; and a planet poisoned by violent global conflicts.

How Joan shapes and inherits an apocalyptic future stems from her belief in Harper's version of events that she witnessed as a child. At nighttime, in her aunt's remote house and unable to sleep, she reports seeing what a child should not have to see: glimpses of her uncle beating up adults and children as he moves them from a lorry to be incarcerated in a shed. Each time Joan questions what she heard or saw, Harper twists the reality of these inhumane acts of violence into a tale of acting for the good of humanity. These are not people suffering or being attacked; the uncle is 'helping them escape', 'giving them shelter' (Churchill 2008: 140). The house is a refuge, a place of succour, Harper claims. But the contradiction that Mouffe observes Derrida detected in the word 'hospitality' whose meaning is derived from 'two words with the same roots: "hospis" (host) and "hostis" (enemy)' (2013: 41), is exposed in her version of events. The 'host' is the 'enemy' of those seeking refuge. And yet, instructed by the adult, the child chooses to believe otherwise; Joan is ultimately convinced

---

[38] Mouffe argues that a multipolar, federal, world order consisting of different political and economic models is more likely to minimise rather than escalate 'violent forms of antagonisms'. This she relates to her concept of 'agonistic' rather than 'antagonistic' conflicts – struggles between adversaries rather than enemies.

by Harper's vision that she will be 'on the side of the people who are putting things right' (2008: 142).

Joan's childhood 'desire to be on the side of what's right' – an aspiration that Churchill explains is shared by all three characters, thus providing another connecting thread between the three, elliptical parts of the play (2008: viii) – is implicated in a totalitarian regime. In part two, Joan and Todd are college-educated workers who fashion *'enormous and preposterous'* hats to be worn by those condemned by the state (2008: 147). That their labour is creative, that the hats are worn/displayed for one parade/live performance before being burned with the bodies (just a few are preserved in museums) again gestures to Churchill's concern with 'the nature of theatre'. The hats, Todd reflects, are 'ephemeral. It's like a metaphor for something or other' (2008: 150). A metaphor for 'life', Joan suggests, but as Todd declares his love for the way 'You make beauty and it disappears', the connection to theatre's ephemerality as an art form is hard to resist (2008: 150).

Furthermore, the absurdly rendered imaging of the hats (art) on those condemned to die heightens the sense of theatre's political attachments to abject subjects (in all senses) and the artistry by which it might form them. Retrieving my hastily scribbled notes penned when I saw the original Royal Court production, I find the following observations about the parade: 'beamed effect with coloured light bulbs – prisoners come forward in chains with heads bent – don't see expressions only the hats – most shocking of all – children in the parade, especially a "tiny tot"'. The power of this scene to shock was widely reported by theatre critics, though as Alastair Macaulay commented, 'the play's real shock is in the way these horrors are *accepted*' (2016: 1577; original emphasis). With its wordless, faceless procession of prisoners, the parade is 'the play's central image that remains': a 'striking theatrical experience' (Brook 1972: 152) that renders a lingering, lasting impression of a dehumanising political order.

'There's a lot wrong with this place', Todd, the experienced hat-maker tells Joan, the novice (2008: 144). Questions about the corruption of the industry infiltrate the ritualised sequences of their hat-making labour. Any possibility of changing the system is contingent on them making a connection to the political setup of the industry. Hence, Churchill shifts attention from the personal is political to the political is personal. This reverse formulation of feminism's recognition that women's experiences of inequality are political (see Section 1) acknowledges that attention also needs to be paid to the impact that the political has on people's daily lives.

In their analysis of 'the costs of daily politics', Brett Q. Ford *et al.* observe that although 'day-to-day political events and controversies often occur far away and revolve around issues that can seem irrelevant to most people's daily lives', such 'distant events can have very personal consequences for the average person' (2023: 1). Drawing on political psychology and affective science, they empirically test their theory that 'daily politics' do have an emotional impact on people's lives – politics of all stripes, left or right. 'A hypothesis about life in the imagery of its action' is how theatre contrastingly makes its case, Churchill explains, as she elaborates on how 'a poetic image is a hypothesis which cannot be proved objectively but only by its value and meaning to its writer and audience' (1960: 447). That a dehumanising political world order is not 'far away' is the hypothesis Churchill tests as her poetic image-making makes palpable the negative emotional impact the regime has on the lives of Joan, Todd and Harper. As Katherine Tozer, who played Joan (the adult), commented: 'the nightmare scenario that Caryl describes is really not that far away at all. We would like to hope and think that it is, but the knock-on effect of blinding oneself to the atrocities that are going on in the garden shed is all too prevalent in society today' (qtd in Roberts 2008: 259).

Firmly focused on their hat-making (in performance, the tap, tap, tapping sounds of their labour punctuated the dialogue), Joan and Todd are desensitised to the plight of the prisoners: a shocking lack of empathy resonates through Joan's regret that the hats are burned along with the bodies;[39] the costs to themselves incurred by working for a corrupt industry blinds Todd to the bigger, dehumanising, political picture. Furthermore, Todd's halting attempts to raise Joan's political-is-personal consciousness with regard to the workplace have a negative emotional impact on their burgeoning relationship. The third sequence in the hat-making section finds the two quarrelling. Joan has tired of Todd repeatedly telling her about his suspicions of corruption: 'if you're going on about it all the time I don't know why you don't do something about it' (Churchill 2008: 146). However, a commitment to act ultimately feels tenuous. By the close of part two, Joan and Todd are still *talking* about exposing corruption in the exploitative industry, but their actions "speak" otherwise: they are starting to make new hats.

Behind the scenes, 'the costs of *nightly* politics' also took its toll on the performers involved in *Far Away*. Performing twice nightly during the initial run at the Royal Court, cast and creatives found themselves doubly immersed in Churchill's dark, dystopian drama. Linda Bassett, who played Harper, describes how 'doing it twice a night did take it out of us actually': 'We used to suffer, we all suffered', coping with 'the horror' that the play depicts (2009: 146). She elaborates: 'The way we clung together – that's why when we went to The

---

[39] Tozer recollects that when she delivered the line expressing Joan's regret about the hats being burned with the bodies, she 'looked straight out into the audience'. 'That floored the audience – I know it did' (qtd in Roberts 2008: 261).

Albery[40] we chose to share that dressing room because it was like we were little people up against this horror. We needed the human warmth of each other just to keep going' (2009: 146). As *Far Away*'s poetic-imaging conveys, without a communal feeling of 'human warmth' the world descends into an apocalyptic nightmare of global enmity.

Moreover, a lack of 'human warmth' has ecological implications for all species – human and non-human. As the blood of those people seeking refuge seeped into the earth around Harper's home, so the natural world became infected with humankind's violent, antagonistic relations. In the final, third part of *Far Away,* the stark reality of what is at stake in a *uni*verse where all nations compete for world domination is conveyed by Churchill's surreal imaging of all living things at war. Seeking the comfort of her husband, Joan returns to her aunt's home as a 'place of safety' (Churchill 2008: 153). But as part one established, the house is host to enmity; a sleeping Joan wakes to the ongoing nightmare of war in which it is no longer possible to know whose side any species is on. The animal "kingdom" has surreally taken on the violent traits of the human race: mallards 'commit rape and they're on the side of the elephants and Koreans' (Churchill 2008: 155); the antlers of deer are weaponised, 'twist into teenagers running down the street' (Churchill 2008: 156). By Harper's anthropomorphic reckoning, only the crocodile is 'always in the wrong', though with their 'unstoppable' killer instinct, Todd would prefer crocodiles to be 'on one of the sides we have alliances with' (Churchill 2008: 155).

The intimacy Joan craves with Todd is no longer possible in a world devoid of feeling for all living things. As *What If If Only*'s spirit of the lost future reminds us, love (the 'beloved') can only survive if the alternative, socially democratic 'future that never happened' happens. And this, Churchill impresses, remains a 'far-away' possibility when forces of global enmity kill the joy of the living, figuratively and literally. Todd has 'shot cattle and children in Ethiopia'; 'gassed mixed troops of Spanish, computer programmers and dogs' (Churchill 2008: 157); on the journey to her husband, Joan 'killed two cats and a child under five so it wasn't that different from a mission' (Churchill 2008: 158). 'Everything's been recruited' (Churchill 2008: 159). Elemental forces are siding with different nations: the weather is on the side of the Japanese; 'Bolivians are working with gravity' (Churchill 2008: 159). Was a river Joan needed to cross on her side, or not? As the Skriker predicted, enmeshed in a web of human-born enmity, nature can no longer be counted on as a life-sustaining force. In sum, this is the eco-apocalyptic

---

[40] *Far Away* transferred to *The Albery Theatre* for its run in London's West End. The venue has since been renamed The Noël Coward Theatre.

future created by the antagonistic relations of a power-hungry, unipolar world in global capitalism's hegemonic grasp.

While the characters are desensitised to acts of violence against all life forms, the opposite must obtain for spectators if *Far Away* is to have a politicising impact. Affective poetry (rather than affective science that Brett *et al*. draw on) is the means by which Churchill resolves the query that *This is a Chair* raises: how to move beyond a Brechtian-influenced mode of political theatre-making. 'It's a poem more than it's a play', Bassett observed of *Far Away*: 'That whole last scene, with all the animals and everything is mind-blowing' (2009: 146). Language is 'distilled and distilled and distilled so that you say one word and its doing the work of four sentences' (2009: 144). Under Stephen Daldry's direction, the poetic distillation of language brought an immersive quality to the play.[41] As a spectator, you needed to feel-think your way through to understanding the eco-tragedy that unfolds. Eco philosopher Timothy Morton reflects how: 'We usually think of ecology as having to do with science and social policy. But as the poet Percy Shelley said, regarding the developments in science, "We want the creative faculty to imagine that which we know"' (2010: 1). Churchill's affective, poetic rendering of a world lost to the dehumanising forces of capitalism, urges a deeper, darker, ecological imagining of what we think or presume to already know. Just as arcadia cannot be thought of in *Fen's* bleak, exploited landscape, so *Far Away* strips away the idea that nature can be conceived 'as a reified thing in the distance' (Morton 2010: 3). The artificial rural idyl depicted on the front cloth at the start of the performance,[42] is what we need to strip away. At the close, the front cloth crashed to the floor; my in-the-moment notes read this sounded 'like a shot or a guillotine'. The execution of all species is the chilling thought that lingers.

One final reflection: the notion of speaking truth to power is often attributed to political theatre. But in the case of *Far Away* I would nuance or put this somewhat differently. Performed against the political backdrop of neoliberal governance, this ecological drama evinced a capacity to bolster our *power to doubt*: to disbelieve that capitalism's hegemonic hold is permanent; that there is no alternative, as the likes of Thatcher and her neoliberal successors would have us believe. As Churchill, by means of her experimentally rendered, politicising feeling structures, impresses on us (her audience) the idea that planetary

---

[41] Daldry previously directed *This is a Chair*. His process that I have referred to a 'physical-actioning', of counterpointing dialogue with gesture or movement, is one that lends itself to the visual and the experiential (Aston 2009: 157). A sense of immersion was also heightened by staging the play in the Royal Court's studio space, rather than the main auditorium; an audience was close up, not 'far away' from the action.

[42] Ian MacNeil designed the cloth. A sense of nature as artifice was also heightened by Paul Arditti's soundscape with its artificially reproduced sounds of birds or water.

survival is highly doubtful in a unipolar, capitalist-committed, antagonistically formed universe, so she potentially elicits a widely shared, if-only yearning for an alternative political order in which the 'future that never happened' happens.

3.3 Renewed Attachments to Socialism and Feminism

A majority of theatre critics accorded *Far Away* a warm reception; a few were less convinced by Churchill's politicising move from the 'real to surreal' (Billington 2000: 1578). But as R. Darren Gobert describes, subsequent to its initial production, *Far Away* 'wormed its way under culture's skin, where like an anxious threat it restively lurks'; it 'is now one of Churchill's most celebrated [and performed] plays' (2014: 38).

A fervent belief in being on the right side of history resurfaces in *Drunk Enough to Say I Love You?* (Royal Court Theatre, 2006), a play in which the idea of being enthralled to a unipolar vision of a world dictated by hostile North American foreign policies spanning the twentieth to twenty-first century is subject to critical scrutiny. A toxic cocktail of love and politics is played with just a cast of two: one character (Sam) represents America and another an ordinary man (Guy). This was not an isolated example of Churchill writing for an all-male cast. *A Number* (Royal Court Theatre, 2002) was an all-male two-hander in which anxieties about advances in reproductive bio-technology find a father in difficult relations with his three cloned sons (the sons all played by the same actor).[43] One might then be tempted to question whether these all-male dramas signal a rupture in Churchill's attachments to feminism. But feminism casts its shadow over *A Number's* troubled patriarchal set-up and the political-is-personal affections for a system of militaristic, masculine aggression that Sam/America embodies in *Drunk Enough to Say I Love You?* As Janelle Reinelt reflects writing on the all-male *Softcops* (1984) – Churchill's earlier, Foucauldian take on surveillance and punishment – 'the absence of women is not an accident: *Softcops* is about a patriarchal culture and its power relations' (1994: 96). In short, such works do have 'profound implications for the feminist project' (1994: 96).

It was at a mid-point in the second decade of the twenty-first century that Churchill resumed her 'feminist project' with an *all-female* cast. Premiered at the Royal Court Theatre in 2016, *Escaped Alone*, with its four roles for older women, appeared at a time of renewed attachments to socialist and feminist politics.

---

[43] Churchill's early radio play *Identical Twins* (1968), another male two-hander, was also staged in 2002 as part of a special series of 'Caryl Churchill Events' marking the thirtieth anniversary of her Royal Court debut with *Owners*.

From Murray's trade-unionist perspective, it was the anti-war protest against American President George W. Bush's invasion of Iraq in February 2003 that began to re-energise the Left. The protest was international, but the UK in particular saw a national upsurge of opposition to Blair's support for Bush: a hitherto dormant socialist left in the trade unions, Labour Party, Communist Party, Socialist Workers Party, joined with those from the peace movement and Muslim communities in forging an anti-war coalition.[44] 'The anti-war movement thus represented the first successful gathering of the "fragments" of the left' (Murray 2019: 87). Although the anti-war, anti-capitalist energies of this movement did not stop the invasion, in the longer term they were significant with regard to the Left's renewal and the 2015 election of socialist Jeremy Corbyn to leader of the Labour Party.

Furthermore, in the wake of the global banking crisis in 2007–2008 austerity measures were deemed necessary to shore up a morally and economically "bankrupt" capitalist system. A 'good government would have looked to protect the weakest', but as Polly Toynbee and David Walker point out, David Cameron's coalition government (2010–15) with its maldistribution of social and economic 'pain' did exactly the opposite (2015: 3). Hence, as social and economic inequalities worsened, so resistance to neoliberal governance in the form of renewed activism and re-energised social movements grew. With regard to feminism, a revitalised movement gained traction in a way that had not been seen since feminism's second wave.[45] This new wave of feminist activism, galvanised mainly by younger generations of women, protested malingering 'patriarchal attitudes', a protest that in 2017 would go viral through the #MeToo movement's call to 'speak bitterness' against misogyny's global reach. Furthermore, anti-capitalist and intersectional in outlook, this revitalised feminist movement also heeded what Churchill had expressed in *Top Girls* as the need to address the social and economic welfare of *all* women.

3.4 *Escaped Alone*: the Political, the Personal, and the Depressive

In contrast to the anti-capitalist momentum generated by younger generations more attached to socialist and/or feminist values than had been the case since the rise of neoliberalism in the 1980s, *Escaped Alone's* generation of older women appear suspended in a state of anxious disquietude, one that the play reveals stems from lives long lived in a world that has failed to transform, socially and ecologically.

The person–political disconnect that Churchill essayed in *This is a Chair* is back, but it runs deeper and darker than before. Three women – Sally, Vi and

---

[44] For details, see Murray 2019: 81–87. [45] For details, see Aston 2020: 5–6.

Lena – are joined by a fourth, Mrs Jarrett (Mrs J), in Sally's backyard where summer afternoons are spent chatting and drinking tea. This personal backyard is a defence against the bigger ecological, political picture. A fence forms a boundary to the yard, and yet it is no defence against a world hurtling towards planetary extinction. Mrs J, a relative outsider to the group, is the 'escaped-alone', solitary figure who, from a void outside of the garden, monologues on scenes of worldwide, apocalyptic destruction. The Royal Court's design of an overly bright garden[46] juxtaposed with and disturbed by Mrs J's appearances on a darkened stage framed by two rectangular frames of pulsing, electric lights, visually reinforced the idea that we cannot escape ecological disaster.

The style of the women's elliptically formed conversations is also indebted to *This is a Chair*, more specifically, its fifth 'Hong Kong' sequence. This was a scene that Churchill originally wrote as a standalone experiment with how little needs to be said to understand what is going on (Churchill 2008: viii). Traces of this experiment are to be found in her subsequent works, notably in the elliptically worded intimacy and quarrelling that shape *Drunk Enough's* love affair with America. This experimentation also accounts for Churchill's long-standing collaboration with *Escaped Alone's* Director James Macdonald, a director who is 'drawn to plays' that he doesn't 'know how to do' – plays that pose a 'directing challenge' and appeal to his attraction to 'puzzles' (qtd in Trueman 2016). In *Escaped Alone*, language is again distilled; but an incomplete sentence, just a word or two, is enough to grasp what the women are talking about – their families, television programmes, or changes to shops on their high streets. These topics are inconsequential, light, and often humorous, in keeping with the ambience of the brightly lit yard.

Yet there are dark undercurrents that belie a sunny disposition. Sally, Vi and Lena all suffer from incapacitating states of anxiety: Sally with her phobia of cats, Lena struggling with agoraphobia after the stresses and strains of a high-powered career, and Vi living with the knowledge that she killed her abusive husband. As I have reflected elsewhere, each of these injurious states represents a dimension of Churchill's eco-socialist-feminist critique: the pressures of the neoliberal workplace (Lena), domestic violence (Vi), and the 'horror' of a predatory world projected on to the feline species that Sally has to keep from invading her house (Aston 2020: 102). The political thus has negative, emotional consequences for women's personal well-being.

It is Mrs J, a role that returned Bassett to another Churchillian dystopia, who bridges the gap between the political and the personal. Her seven monologues disrupt each of the play's eight backyard scenes as she reports on a world

---

[46] The designer was Miriam Buether; Peter Mumford designed the lighting.

plagued by catastrophes. Like the messenger in the biblical story of Job, she reports on one disaster after another. Except, this is not man's faith in a Christian God being tested at the behest of Satan, but his faith in the Satanic forces of global capitalism. Capitalism is adept at evading responsibility for and the consequences of the damage it inflicts – or rather, its political pundits are, as evinced in the bankers' bail-out in the 2007–2008 crash and the consequent austerity measures that were punitive to the poor, rather than the arbiters of the economic disaster. But capitalism as the harbinger and agent of social, economic and ecological disaster is exposed in Mrs J's surreal, poetically voiced reckonings: it was 'senior executives' who paid for the 'four hundred thousand tons of rock' that 'split off the hillside to smash through the roofs, each fragment onto the designated child's head' (Churchill 2016: 8); it was 'chemicals leaked through cracks in the money' that caused fatal illnesses (Churchill 2016: 17); it was 'wind developed by property developers' that 'turned heads inside out' (Churchill 2016: 28). Absurd and yet 'intricately wired into current politics' (Clapp 2016: 63), these catastrophes appear strangely familiar. Delivered by Bassett in a dissociative tone, the monologues cumulatively attest to the stupidity that *What If If Only*'s ghost of the dead future decries as our failure to choose differently.

Time is running out to make a different choice. The summer afternoon that passes is in fact, Churchill instructs, '*a number of afternoons*' (Churchill 2016: 4) that grow darker; the Aristotelian unity of time passing 'within a single revolution of the sun' is distorted (Aristotle 1965: 38). In Churchillian dramatic landscapes time more often than not proves tricksterish, as exemplified by *The Skriker* where Lily's eco-tragic downfall is her belief that time will stand still while she accompanies the Skriker to her underworld. Instead, as noted in Section 2, she finds herself in the 'cemetery, a black whole hundred yearns' later (Churchill 1994: 52). In *Far Away*, time passes between the three parts, but each episode links to a unified action: the war of all against all that is not a 'black whole hundred yearns' hence, but in the present time of global capitalism. And in *Escaped Alone*, planetary destruction is neither in the present nor the future, but in the past: it has already happened. Mrs J's monologic cataloguing of catastrophic events consists of reports, not predictions.

As the 'black whole' of the void parallels the garden, so the state of the planet appears critical and urgent. Yet the women are paralysed by their heightened states of respective anxiety. In the Royal Court production, the ensemble was suspended, frozen, as each woman in the garden vocalised her anxiety-ridden phobia of cats, kitchens, or going outside. Lena, in her depressive, agoraphobic state, tells us: 'I sat on the bed this morning and didn't stand up till lunchtime'.

She finds it hard to breathe meaning or purpose into her daily life: 'The air was too thick. It's hard to move, it's hard to see why you'd move' (Churchill 2016: 32).

'What political emotions can be glimpsed in accounts of depression?', asks Hannah Proctor in her highly illuminating *Burnout: The Emotional Experience of Political Defeat*. 'Is it possible to think political transformation and emotional paralysis as enmeshed rather than antithetical? Could the airless space paradoxically ventilate utopia?' (2024: 73). These are questions Proctor poses when reflecting on second-wave feminism and its aftermath in relation to her overarching concern with the negative emotions that arise when social movements fail to achieve their revolutionary goals.[47]

In *Escaped Alone* there is no feminist backstory to the play's septuagenarian women; they are not portrayed as disappointed, defeated revolutionaries. But generationally, they are of an age (like Churchill) to have lived through the years when revolutionary change felt possible, the decades of 'political defeat', and a world-ending, dystopian present. Does this political backdrop mean that in their state of personal, depressive paralysis, the spark of utopic feminist feeling is extinguished? Or does the 'air' that is 'too thick' 'ventilate utopia'?

In one sense, the 'emotional paralysis' Churchill depicts in *Escaped Alone* feels 'antithetical' to the structures of revolutionary, feminist feeling she captured in her wave of 1970s feminist theatre. And yet, despite the women's individual anxieties, a feeling of shared resilience is 'enmeshed' in their spirited afternoon socials. This is not a consciousness-raising feminist collective, but neither is it an all-female gathering in which women talk over and fail to listen to each other, *à la Top Girls*. It is an affirmative, supportive group without which the likes of Lena would not get out of bed at all. There can be the odd barbed comment or difference of opinion, but care-giving is paramount. For instance, we learn that it is Sally who came to Vi's defence when she was tried for the murder of her husband, choosing not to 'tell it quite how it was' because of 'what he was like' (Churchill 2016: 34). Although Vi feels resentful about her friend thinking of her as a murderer, it is the women's allegiance to each other that has served as a defence against an abusive patriarchy.

During waves of activism, Proctor observes that a political commitment to revolutionary goals often comes at the expense of emotional well-being: agitating for change takes its psychological toll, impacting not only the energies to keep up the struggles but also interpersonal relations within movements. Hence,

---

[47] Proctor's chapter on 'Depression' explores the shift from the political to the depressive in the works and lives of second-wave iconic figures Shulamith Firestone and Kate Millett. The descriptor 'airless spaces' is the title of Firestone's 1997 autobiographical account of mental breakdown.

affective care-giving is essential to social movements 'fighting against oppressive and exploitative social conditions even when victory seems remote' (Proctor 2024: 2). But attention also needs to be paid to emotional well-being in between waves of activism: to what Proctor, citing Lisa Baraitser, identifies as a different time: 'the slowness of chronic time, rather than the time of rupture; the durational drag of staying alongside others, rather than the time of transgression' (Proctor 2024: 2). This is the time *Escaped Alone's* women occupy: 'the durational drag of staying alongside' each other as the afternoons pass, not the 'time of rupture' that fuelled Churchill's *Vinegar Tom* or *Light Shining in Buckinghamshire*.

This does not mean that political anger is extinguished. Mrs J's one and only monologue in the garden (rather than the void) renders palpable her hitherto suppressed anger at all the atrocities she has witnessed and reported on as she repeats the word 'rage' twenty-five times (Churchill 2016: 42). But to emotionally sustain political anger through 'rupture' and 'defeat', to keep on keeping on with the struggles for social transformation at the risk of 'burnout', requires care of the inner self, personal and interpersonal well-being. And as *Escaped Alone* depicts, in the 'durational drag of staying alongside others', restorative, reparative pleasures are necessary: a song the women chorus in the garden they sing '*for themselves*', '*not performing to the audience*' (Churchill 2016: 28). The Crystals' 'Da Doo Ron Ron' was Churchill's choice of song for the production;[48] a utopic, joyous note pierced the canvas of a dystopian world still yet to be transformed. In short, holding on to political anger but also taking care of each other, not letting go of 'human warmth', is the wisdom that Churchill's older generation of women pass on to those younger generations agitating for change and those social movements still to come.

For a veteran political theatre maker such as Churchill, burnout is also a risk. Although theatre critics often point out that her powers of creative invention remain undiminished (a view that I share), how to form politicising dramatic landscapes across shifting times of 'rupture' and 'defeat' can take its toll, as evinced at the time of her 'this-is-not-a play' period in the late 1990s. Equally, performing her dark, dystopian drama can also be a draining experience, as Bassett observed in relation to *Far Away*. And just as *Escaped Alone's* women are sensitive to each other's welfare, so Churchill also has to have a care for her audience's emotional experience: to leave the theatre feeling that the world is beyond saving is to kill the belief in and hope for an alternative future. Thus, however thick the dystopian air in her plays, she always seeks

---

[48] Bassett explained: 'It was Caryl who suggested the Crystals. When we were touring her play *Fen*, we drove around the country in a minibus and used to sing it a lot. Caryl remembered that. It's the best song ever!' (qtd in Wiegand 2016).

ways to breathe life into the idea that there can be an alternative, as Section 4 will amplify and substantiate.

4 Towards a Theatre of 'Anti-Adaptive Healing'

In an elliptical, associative language reminiscent of the Skriker, *What If If Only*'s ghost of the egalitarian future that never happened explains that there were 'so many so many futures that didn't happen like drops of rain grains of sand atoms in your heart' (Churchill 2021: 10). Someone's grieving and craving for their dead 'beloved' conjures up those futures that never happened, for better or worse. Imagine if the war had been lost and Someone never existed because their 'parents were never born' (Churchill 2021: 11). Or think of the 'fright' because the future might have been 'nuclear' (Churchill 2021: 11). Imagine too if the colonial gears of history had shifted – 'no rule the waves no slaves' (Churchill 2021: 11). Most striking of all is the way these lost-future voicings enable the planet to talk back: 'if only you hadn't driven and guzzled and poisoned me me you'd have tigers and coral' and 'the seas the seas full of fish' (Churchill 2021: 11). From the earth's point of view, the extinction of the human race might have been the best ecological solution: 'if only wiped you all out eek eeek solved your problem' (Churchill 2021: 11).

Such 'what if' and 'if only' voicings demonstrate that futures are not fixed but fluid; the course of history can change. And yet, the ghost of the lost egalitarian future laments that 'enemies say I'm utopia a nowhere place' (Churchill 2021: 10). Churchill's insistence that change is possible, that an eco-socialist-feminist future can be a utopian *somewhere* rather than a 'nowhere place' is a key consideration in this concluding, fourth section.

Writing in a utopian tradition, Troy Vettese and Drew Pendergrass in *Half-Earth Socialism: A Plan to Save the Future from Extinction, Climate Change, and Pandemics* (2022), map out what they envision as an eco-socialist future. To make their case for the necessity and possibility of this utopian future, they begin in an opposite way by imagining the dystopian future that awaits if capitalism persists, and eco-socialist formations fail to materialise.[49] Emulating Vettese and Pendergrass' strategy, I turn first to the dystopian mode of Churchill's 1971 radio drama *Not Not Not Not Not Enough Oxygen* (hereafter abbreviated to *Not Enough Oxygen*) and thereafter to the utopian impulse of *Cloud Nine*, first staged by the Joint Stock theatre company in 1979. Returning to the 1970s after the chronological mapping of the previous three

---

[49] Fundamental to the utopian future Vettese and Pendergrass envisage is the re-wilding of half the earth (to stabilise the biosphere) and a socialist order (in the interests of a 'better society') (2022: loc. 168). They argue that environmental reforms alone will not resolve the ecological crisis; capitalism must also be addressed as an eco-socially damaging form.

sections affords a final, retrospective viewing of Churchill's abiding concern with capitalism's unmaking of alternative futures *and* the possibility of making those futures that did not happen, happen. In brief, the segue and contrast between *Not Enough Oxygen* and *Cloud Nine* will serve to illuminate how dystopian criticality is twinned with the utopic impulse to desire and live differently.

In turn, this focus on dystopian critique and desiring differently paves the way for a summative understanding of Churchill's theatre as a site of 'anti-adaptive healing'. The concept of 'anti-adaptive healing' is conceived by Hannah Proctor in *Burn Out* (2024). As explained in Section 3, Proctor is concerned with the psychological toll of surviving both in and beyond political struggles. She proposes 'anti-adaptive healing' as a way to acknowledge and address the 'contradictory relationships between the transformative and the restorative, between revolution and healing, between rupture and repair' (2024: 16). Thinking of these 'contradictory relationships', I return to *What If If Only* to offer a summation of Churchill's theatre as engaging us – her spectators and readers – in anti-adaptive, resistant feelings towards a dystopian, capitalist order and healing through a utopian sensing that an alternative future is desirable and still possible.

4.1 Dystopian Critique: *Not Not Not Not Not Enough Oxygen*

Raymond Williams observed that the 'systematic dystopia' was far more prevalent in the twentieth century than its utopian counterpart (1983: 12), an observation that also obtains for the early twenty-first century given a heightened sense of ecological crisis and fear of planetary extinction that no longer feels 'far away'.[50] This is the crisis Churchill prophesied more than half a century ago. In 1971, *Not Enough Oxygen* broadcast a world that, as the title of the play indicates, is so polluted it is impossible to breathe; its oxygen-deprived characters struggle to complete fully formed sentences.[51] The year is 2010 and the place is London, or more precisely, the play text refers to 'the Londons', plural (Churchill 1990b: 42), implicating financial cities the world over as major pollutants. You need money to survive in this dystopian universe where food and water are rationed, and meat is only available if you can pay for it. It is a Malthusian world in which births are also "rationed" – regulated by permits.

---

[50] Siân Adiseshiah observes that 'dystopian cultural production – novels, films, TV, drama – is now everywhere' to the extent that it risks losing the power to be critically impactful. However, she singles out dystopian plays from the subsidised, new-writing, theatre sector for their capacity to 'retain dystopian criticality'. Among her examples are Churchill's *Far Away* and *Escaped Alone* (2023: 4).

[51] The play aired on BBC 3, 31 March 1971.

We hear that outside of the residential tower blocks, whose inhabitants are confined to a one-room, walled-in existence, green spaces are vanishing, the skies are empty of birds, and the air-polluted streets are raging with so-called fanatics – those without means of survival who protest, kill, or kill themselves. Hence, this dystopian drama reveals capitalism's "breath taking" capacity to produce planetary extinction.

If there is to be a utopian turn, then the future cannot belong to capitalism. As Vettese and Pendergrass argue in their utopian schematics, to understand and redress the environmental crisis you also have to comprehend and change 'the structure of the society that caused it' (2022: loc. 1035). Thus, time and again, in *The Skriker, Far Away* or *Escaped Alone*, Churchill impresses the need for us to recognise capitalism for the eco-socially damaging force that it is. That capitalism pollutes and commodifies the very air that we breathe crystallises in this flashpoint from *Not Enough Oxygen*: a young woman, Vivian, sprays the room of her older lover, Mick, with oxygen from a bottle that is not freely available but has to be paid for. Like the bottle of perfume Marlene gifts to her sister in *Top Girls*, which Angie insists Joyce liberally sprays over them all (Churchill 1990a: 122), the oxygen bottle sprays the "scent" of money. My note on the spraying of oxygen in the 2002 staging of *Not Enough Oxygen* at the Royal Court as part of a series of 'Caryl Churchill Events', reads that there was a 'ludicrous feel to this gesture'.[52] But from the retrospective vantage point of our post-pandemic era, this prescient imaging of an airless, oxygen-deprived world no longer feels absurd given the shortage and maldistribution of life-saving oxygen during the height of the Covid-19 pandemic.[53]

Prescient too was Churchill's critical sensing of how capitalism's hegemonic grasp is bolstered by what Stuart Hall described as the way in which people's political views are impacted by 'ceaseless massaging by the media' and the '"disinformation" from the politicians' – a relentless 'game of impression-management' (1988: 260). In *Not Enough Oxygen*, the mediatised view of the 'madness they say sweeping the country sweeping all the countries' (Churchill 1990b: 48) is attributed to those violently opposed to a capitalist world where

---

[52] Furthermore, in the Court's staging of the play, a moment in which Vivian and Mick open a window in an attempt to oxygenate their airless room was enacted by opening a window of the studio theatre. The rumbling sounds of London traffic became audible; Churchill's futuristic imagining of 'the Londons' in 2010 that by 2002 was only a few years away, coalesced with the reality of the air-polluting traffic outside.

[53] Vivian's nighttime fear that 'the block is going to go up to go up in flames any any any any moment go up' (Churchill 1990b: 43) also resonates all the more strongly given the Grenfell Tower disaster (June 2017). This national tragedy occurred when the Grenfell social-housing block in North Kensington, London, was destroyed over night by a fire that spread rapidly due to renovation work that had deployed highly combustible cladding, resulting in the deaths of 72 people.

people are starving – the so-called fanatics. These are the voiceless others whose violence "speaks" of the dispossession that capitalism refuses to notice or to hear.[54] Vettese and Pendergrass reflect that when 'Capital is at the helm blindly steering the ship of fools towards ecological disaster', it cannot 'feel the wind or listen to its shouting passengers.' It is guided only by 'price signals' and hence 'destroys the world it cannot see' (2022: loc. 732). And as Churchill portrays in *Not Enough Oxygen*, when capitalism cannot 'feel' – is de-sensitised to – the elemental forces of nature and fails to hear the angry shouts of those it dispossesses, then the critical question that arises is how to steer a different, alternative course?

Citing Marx's notion of capital as an '"automatic subject", an unconscious force' (2022: loc. 701), Vettese and Pendergrass propose that 'socialism must be the restoration of human consciousness as a historical force' (2022: loc. 732). In *Not Enough Oxygen*, the 'restoration of a human consciousness' resides with Mick's estranged son, Claude. A wealthy, celebrated, young musician, Claude has opted to give away his millions and join the ranks of the dispossessed rather than, as he puts it, 'kill anyone else' (Churchill 1990b: 53). There will be no happy reunion of father and son; no gifting of money by Claude to ease the zombie-like, living-dead existence his father clings to. Utopian sensibilities of the feminist kind are generated by this leave-taking of the paternal since Claude's exit from the capitalist order means following his mother's example of leaving behind a life dictated by possessions and money. This was the mother who Claude says 'gave up all her things. Not that she had much, she never – Tried to give her – when I first earned – but she wouldn't' (Churchill 1990b: 47). We do not know whether his absent, unseen mother has survived, and death apparently awaits the dispossessed Claude. But mother and son's conscious eschewal of capitalism is a reparative gesture – one that implicates feminism and socialism as the coordinates of an alternative, more politically hopeful future. As *What If If Only*'s ghost reminds us, choosing differently means that the future can be different. And for Churchill, as evinced by my analysis of her theatre over the course of this Element, this necessitates choosing an ecologically aware, socialist feminism.

4.2 Desiring Differently: *Cloud Nine*

In the dystopic universe of *Not Enough Oxygen*, the necessity of choosing differently is confined to a utopian gesture towards ecological and social

---

[54] In the years to come, Churchill will repeatedly oppose the mediatised idea of a fanatical Left – the pejorative imaging of 'the "loony left"' (Hall 1988: 263). Rather, in a Churchillian landscape, the fanatics will be those crazed by capitalism: Marion, the mentally unstable capitalist zealot in *Owners*; the frenetic greedy moneymakers in *Serious Money*; or Sam/U.S.A. thirsty for world domination in *Drunk Enough to Say I Love You?*

redemption. But in the utopian-themed *Cloud Nine*, Churchill shifts her attention to the counter-cultural dynamics of making an alternative future happen. In the first of the play's two acts set in colonial Africa during the Victorian era, gender-fluid desires propel an Ortonesque-styled critique of patriarchalism and colonialism. Slipping through a Skriker-like time warp, in the second act, characters emerge in London one hundred years later as a kind of counter-hegemonic-styled grouping through which a utopian desire for sexual liberation is expressed.

Writing on the utopian, Williams distinguished between the formation of 'utopian desire' and the 'schematic utopia'. The former he characterised as 'an imaginative encouragement to feel and to relate differently, or to strengthen and confirm existing feelings and relationships which are not at home in the existing order and cannot be lived through it' (1983: 13). The latter he explained 'can envisage, in general structure but also in detail, a different and practical way of life' (1983: 13). Both are relevant to Churchill's comedically rendered 'cloud-nine' antics that are invested in transforming the 'existing order'.

In Act One, it is the formation of 'utopian desire' that primarily drives the action: the desire to desire differently sees colonised sexualities rebelling against a patriarchal, colonial and heteronormative system. With the exception of the white, patriarch, Clive, none of the characters 'feel at home in the existing order'. The opening tableau of the family gathered around the British flag in which Clive's son is played by a woman, his wife by a man, his Black servant by a white actor, and his daughter by a doll, demonstrates that none of the assembled can be what the patriarch wants them to be. They may sing in praise of 'old England' as their "home" but their misaligned bodies "voice" a state of non-belonging (Churchill 1985: 251). The colonial and patriarchal power invested in Clive is slipping and keeps on slipping throughout the act as his unruly "subjects" refuse to conform. Just as the dystopian *Not Enough Oxygen* urges liberation from an eco-damaging capitalism, so *Cloud Nine* sees the death of colonial and patriarchal power (Clive is murdered by his Black servant at the close of the act) as also critical to the liberation of feminist, queer, and decolonialised futures.[55]

And yet, in and of itself, desiring differently is not enough to make those futures happen. What is involved in turning the world upside down comes to the fore in Act Two, where the focus is on the inner workings of the counter-cultural regrouping of the characters[56], and which utopian schematics are to co-ordinate

---

[55] On Churchill's critique of colonialism, see also her early play, *The Hospital at the Time of the Revolution* inspired by and partly based on Frantz Fanon's *The Wretched of the Earth*. Play text published in *Churchill: Shorts* (Churchill 1990b).

[56] That Churchill dramatizes a kind of collective, counter-cultural grouping is significant with regard to acting for change. Recollect, for instance, that Lilly's *individual* act of kindness

their 'cloud-nine' future. To be clear, this act does not take the form of a 'schematic utopia', rather it playfully dramatises the characters in the *process* of striving to transform 'utopia a nowhere place' into a *somewhere*. This proves to be far from straightforward. There are personal experiences and interpersonal differences to negotiate, dramatisations of which were in part influenced by the way that the workshop on sexual politics for *Cloud Nine* involved members of the Joint Stock company processing their own 'different attitudes and experiences' (Churchill 1985: 245). Furthermore, intellectual approaches to understanding sexual politics are not necessarily put into practice. For instance, Martin, the husband of Victoria (Clive's daughter), a figuration of the new man that was the butt of much women's humour,[57] 'has all the theory of having given [power] up while keeping it in practice' (Churchill qtd in Roberts 2008: 200). Churchill elaborates: 'he has all his sexual politics in the head, doesn't mean harm, means quite well with nasty flashes, but is so used to being in charge that he finds it hard to stop and talks Vic [Victoria] into the ground with what is meant to be the politics of her freedom' (Churchill qtd in Roberts 2008: 200). As Hannah Proctor elucidates, change calls for what she terms 'patient urgency': recognition of the 'asynchronicity of individual and social transformation – the fact that people's behaviours and desires often fail to transform at the pace demanded by their political ideals' (2024: 28). Evolving relations between Victoria and her would-be lesbian lover and single mum, Lin, also evince the tension between the urgent desire for queer-feminist transformation and the slower-paced process of changing personal behaviours. Churchill explained that, akin to Martin, Victoria's 'feminism and politics are all in books and the head and it takes her relationship with Lin to loosen them up and make them real' (Churchill qtd in Roberts 2008: 200). Equally, while Lin catches a 'bit of theory from Vic [Victoria]' (Churchill qtd in Roberts 2008: 201), this does not mean that all aspects of her life change at once. 'I've changed who I sleep with, I can't change everything', Lin remonstrates with Victoria (Churchill 1985: 303). 'Like when I had to stop you getting a job in a boutique and collaborating with sexist consumerism', Victoria responds (Churchill 1985: 303).

With regard to utopian, feminist schematics, there are many details to work out in theory and practice. Socialist-feminist politics provided the analysis that urges the revolutionary transformation of the family in the interests of women's

---

towards the Skriker when she agrees to accompany the spirit to her underworld, is not enough to save the planet. See also Churchill's Monty Pythonesque television play, *The After-Dinner Joke*, broadcast on BBC 1 in 1978, in which the solo efforts of a young woman to do charitable, good works on an international scale come hopelessly undone because of political and corporate business interests. Play text published in *Churchill: Shorts* (Churchill 1990b).

[57] The joke was that in reality the much-vaunted reincarnation of the family man who took an equal share of housework and childcare did not exist.

domestic and work-based lives (see discussion of *Top Girls* in Section 2), but how to revolutionise the family at the individual, personal level? Betty, Clive's wife, who, after leaving her husband, is processing and changing her conservative social attitudes and sexual behaviour, observes: 'if there isn't a right way to do things you have to invent one' (Churchill 1985: 319). Inventing an alternative queer-feminist household involves unsettling the familial norm that Martin, Victoria and their child, Tommy, represent. It requires negotiating childcare arrangements, work, and sexual desires, as the embryonically formed collective housing Lin, her daughter Cathy, Victoria, Tommy and Edward, Victoria's gay brother, demonstrates. Arrangements are not fixed but remain fluid: Betty may or may not be part of their household in the future; Victoria is due to leave London for a new job in Manchester; and Edward is re-connecting with his former lover, Gerry. In brief, the utopian-orientated, queer-feminist dynamics of this act serve not to map out a fully formed 'schematic utopia' but to endorse what Williams identifies as one of its strengths: its affirmation of 'the belief that human beings can live in radically different ways, by radically different values, in radically different kinds of social order' (1983: 13).

Holding on to that 'belief' is vital since the 'enemies' of a politically hopeful future prevail, as evinced in this flashpoint: Act Two Scene Three's nighttime, drunken orgy in the park where Victoria, Edward, and Lin attempt to conjure up a goddess from ancient times, 'before Christ, before men drove [her] out and burnt [her] temples' (1985: 308). In the midst of drunken laughter and polymorphous sexual overtures, Edward and Lin join Victoria in chanting: 'give us back what we were, give us the history we haven't had, make us the women we can't be' (1985: 308). But no goddess appears, only men. First Martin and then the ghost of a soldier (Lin's brother) killed in Northern Ireland – a haunting reminder of colonialism and sexism. As Churchill explains, the ghost of the soldier represents 'The last bit of empire, "fucking" as sex and aggression, a man's life, his anger and pain at what he's been through, and real yearning for something else at the end' (qtd in Roberts, 2008: 202). What he yearns for is 'a fuck', that's why he has come back (Churchill 1985: 311). A function of ghosts, Proctor elucidates, is that they 'make demands and produce a "something-to-be-done", which opens up possibilities for the future' (2024: 171). Raging against 'Man's fucking life in the fucking army' (Churchill 1985: 311), the ghost of the soldier releases a 'something-to-be-done' feeling about the vestiges of a militaristic colonialism. While colonial and sexual aggression continue to weigh heavily on the present, the living cannot resurrect the archaic goddess that would enable the women (and Edward who is discovering his "feminine" side) to become what they still cannot be. Hence, what this flashpoint encapsulates is the idea that counter-cultural, counter-hegemonic formations of desiring differently have to contend with the persistence of old, hegemonic systems and values oppositional to an alternative future.

Nonetheless, as *Cloud Nine* overall exemplifies, the possibility of change rests with the struggles of those who are discounted by or do not 'feel at home in the existing order'. And that, as Hall observes in his reflections on the counter-hegemonic struggles against an existing 'hegemonic system' is 'the reason why history is never closed but maintains an open horizon towards the future' (2011: 728).

Overall, this brief, side-by-side re-viewing of *Not Enough Oxygen* and *Cloud Nine* demonstrates the fundamental choice Churchill insists (and persists in stating over the decades) that we need to make. Either, like Mick and Vivian, we cling to a zombie-like existence under an order that capitalises nature and augurs planetary extinction. Or we desire differently and believe in the reparative possibility of living a radically different way of life. As Françoise d'Eaubonne succinctly and starkly stated in the title of her pioneering eco-feminist study (discussed in Section 1), the choice is between 'Feminism or Death'.

4.3 *What If If Only*: A Theatre of 'Anti-Adaptive Healing'

As my chronological triptych attests, Churchill the political playwright has had to contend with what Proctor sub-titles 'the emotional experience of political defeat' – the loss over the decades of alternative, 'cloud-nine' futures. Hence, the Skriker-like, dark ecological future portrayed in Churchill's recent work might suggest that a radical alternative to "death" under neoliberalism's relentless regimes of ecological and social damage now appears hope-less. And yet, as *What If If Only* demonstrates, the desire to desire differently lingers as a haunting refrain to the deepening dystopic realities Churchill portrays. Returning one last time to *What If If Only* – the play that inspired, ghosts and frames this Element – affords a concluding exemplification of Churchill's trenchant commitment to eco-socialist-feminist values, her undiminished capacity for experimentation, and my summative proposal to consider Churchill's theatre as a site of 'anti-adaptive healing'.

In *What If If Only*, Someone, alone before the ghost arrives, reflects on reading about a man who devoted years to painting an apple up until the moment he died. More specifically, he 'spent ten years trying to paint an apple so it looked just like an apple' and another 'seven years trying to paint an apple so it looked nothing like an apple' (Churchill 2021: 6). Which form will serve to animate the still life painting of the fruit? The more Someone reflects on this artistry, the more complex it appears: there are so many varieties of apples, so which did the artist choose? And was the fruit painted in a 'perfectly ripe' or decaying, 'rotten' state (Churchill 2021: 7)?

Painting the same subject over and over in differing ways to produce altered states of perception on the part of artist and viewer is an object lesson in experimentation. Analogously, Churchill has returned time and again to facets of the dystopic world that is, but always with an experimental, politicising eye to us seeing and desiring differently. She also shares the painter's interest in still life, non-human subjects: the ecological dimensions of her work urge us to consider our human perceptions of and relations with non-human species and the natural world. As Churchill, through her formally innovative modes of political theatre-making, repeatedly depicts the world in its ecologically and socially 'rotten' state, so she invites us to perceive a world that, in the Skriker's words, is 'hurting, hurt very badly' (Churchill 1994: 31). That perception might 'hurt' us, but also heal through a restorative, it-does-not-have-to be-this-way feeling, as voiced by *What If If Only*'s ghost of the lost egalitarian future. Hence my proposal to reflect on Churchill's theatre as a site of 'anti-adaptive healing'.

As headlined in my introductory remarks, 'anti-adaptive healing' is conceived by Proctor. For Proctor, 'anti-adaptive healing' designates how 'the psychological toll of political struggle necessitates contending with the contradictory relationships between the transformative and the restorative, between revolution and healing, between rupture and repair' (2024: 16). On the one hand, she deploys it to explore 'the contradictory endeavour of striving to heal psychic wounds in a wounded and wounding social reality (without affirming its structures in the process)' (2024: 16). On the other, she also considers 'the psychic damage that can be incurred by fighting to transform social reality (so as to make it less psychically wounding)' (2024: 16). Transposed to the context of Churchill's theatre, 'anti-adaptive healing' is a way to elucidate how Churchill's dramatisations of a 'wounded and wounding social reality' may wound us in their viewing (and reading), while also eliciting 'anti-adaptive' feelings towards the dystopic 'social reality' that is, and a 'healing' sense that the world can be otherwise. In brief, hers is a theatre that potentially generates 'anti-adaptive', resistant feelings towards the dystopic, ecologically and socially damaged world created by capitalism (the perception of which may 'wound'), but heals through the utopian impulse to desire differently.

In *What If If Only*, when the futures that might have been vanish, Someone is left to face the Present. 'Do you like me?' Present asks Someone. 'I'm not very nice not altogether' (Churchill 2021: 12). There are 'So many people sick and dead and crazy from what I'm like' (Churchill 2021: 12). This is a 'wounded and wounding social reality': this is the Present we have inherited because of stupidly failing, as the ghost of the lost egalitarian future reminds us, to choose differently. Here again, Churchill's double-eye viewing is critical to reconnecting the personal to the political. The unnamed Someone could be anyone of us coping with personal grief, especially at the height of the pandemic; it is the ghost who connects Someone and *us* to the bigger political picture. The highly recognisable, shell-shocked feeling of private anguish is, then, the catalyst for probing the alternative future histories that might have been. When these are vanquished, banished from the scene, the Present asks Someone if they can 'feel me now?' (Churchill 2021: 13). As this Element demonstrates throughout, for audiences to *feel* the dystopic worlds created through the loss of ecological, socialist and feminist values is core to Churchill's political theatre-making.

If *What If If Only* 'wounds' us in our viewing or reading, it is because we are sensorially ensnared by Churchill's poetic imagination into feeling-perceiving the ecological and social damage of the world that is now. There is no wordy, political treatise explaining what has gone wrong. If theatre is to move us to feel-see differently then, as Churchill reflected, this depends on the 'power of concentration' that she deemed 'essential to drama' (1960: 450). And that, she surmised, requires theatre not to present a 'literal copy of life but an image, where action is used with the same poetic logic as words in a poem' (1960: 450). Condensed and elliptical, *What If If Only* 'wounds' as it touches us with its poetic imaging of the lost ecologically sustainable and democratic futures – 'Equality and cake and no bad bits at all' (Churchill 2021: 10).

To critically sense a world that is 'hurting hurt very badly', may also generate 'anti-adaptive' feelings – the sense that we no longer want to keep on adapting to the kind of death-like, dystopian existence portrayed in *Not Enough Oxygen*. A resistant, 'anti-adaptive' mode of spectatorship is one that Churchill repeatedly has sought to form, whether by means of the Brechtian feeling structures she formerly deployed, or the elliptical-poetic shape-shifting that characterises her later work. Her dramatic formations of 'anti-adaptive', affectively realised perceptions of a world that does not transform socially or ecologically, are those which potentially give rise to the politicising, 'something-to-be-done' feeling.

And yet, to be 'wounded' by the vision of a world 'hurting hurt very badly' is no guarantee of an 'anti-adaptive' desire to desire differently and to act for change. As Brett Q. Ford *et al.* point out, although a negative emotional response to a 'problematic status quo' may 'encourage citizens to take effective political action and reshape the political system that evoked the negative emotions in the first place', regulation strategies that people deploy to cope with the chronic stresses a political order generates, may militate against them desiring and acting for change (2023: 2). To exemplify: on the ecological front, for instance, emotion regulation might occur when we allay our fears of impending planetary destruction by convincing ourselves that things are not as bad as scientists or politicians would have us believe. Hence, Ford *et al.* propose that 'to effectively harness people's negative emotions', those engaged in social movements 'need people to *not* reduce those emotions, and may even want to increase these emotions' (2023: 23; original emphasis).

Similarly, a Churchillian mode of 'anti-adaptive' spectatorship involves heightening the negative emotions generated by a problematical existing order, thereby optimising the potential to rupture audiences' emotional attachments to those socio-political structures that cause utmost social and ecological damage – primarily, as *Not Enough Oxygen* and *Cloud Nine* jointly evince, capitalism, patriarchalism, and colonialism. Among the plays selected for this study recollect: the songs that intensify speaking bitterness against patriarchy in *Vinegar Tom*; the Skriker's schizophrenic-like language that discharges enmity towards the master race; or the horrific, by turns horrifically funny, reports by Mrs J in *Escaped Alone* that heighten a critical sensing of capitalism's planetary destruction. In performance, emotional intensity depends not just on Churchill's innovative playwriting, but also on the craft of the performers and creatives she collaborates with: the democratically organised ensembles of Monstrous Regiment and Joint Stock; her collaborations with Second Stride's dancers and choreographer Ian Spink, and the long-standing relations she has with all those at the Royal Court Theatre, with its reputation for nurturing contemporary playwriting resistant to a 'problematic status quo'. Her collaborators are those who are majorly drawn to what director James Macdonald describes as an attraction to 'plays that push the boat out in terms of both content and form, plays that take risks or do something bold with language' (qtd in Trueman 2016). In sum, to participate in the making of Churchill's theatre is to be involved in fulfilling her mantra that theatre should 'not be ordinary', 'not be safe' (Churchill 1960: 451).

The emotional journey rendered through Churchill's bold experimentations can be a draining experience for her theatre makers, as Linda Bassett observed in the case of *Far Away* when performers needed the human warmth that came from sharing a dressing room to recuperate from the apocalyptic fabric and feeling of the play (see Section 3).[58] However, for audiences, the negative emotionality of her work is offset, artistically and politically, by its reparative

---

[58] Comparably, in the case of activists in social movements where experiencing an intensification of negative emotions may impact a sense of well-being, Ford *et al.* also counsel the need for ways to 'bolster well-being *after* an action has taken place' (2023: 23; original emphasis). This resonates with what Proctor advocates as the necessity to acknowledge and address 'the psychic damage that can be incurred by fighting to transform social reality' (2024: 16). Churchill's dramatization of this kind of 'psychic damage' is palpable in her short play *The Hospital at the Time of the Revolution*, as referred to in note 55.

dimensions. In terms of Churchill's artistry, it is her theatrical inventiveness that energises rather than depresses (in all senses) our engagement with her subject matter. For instance, again talking of *Far Away*, Bassett wondered how it was that spectators did not find the play 'too bleak': 'they'd say, well the subject matters bleak but the form of expression is exciting, so it's not a depressing experience watching it, it's enlivening' (2009: 146–147). Thus, she concludes that the 'power' of Churchill's 'language' is the reason 'why the audience don't despair' (2009: 147).

Politically and significantly, the reparative also resides in Churchill's trenchant resistance to the idea that change is not possible, as neoliberal governance, especially would have us believe. An 'anti-adaptive' mode of spectatorship is not only against the ecologically and socially damaged world that is, but also *for* the hopeful possibility of an alternative, socially democratic and ecologically sustainable future. Within the fictional worlds of Churchill's plays, that possibility may be foreclosed. The failed revolution in *Light Shining*; women persecuted as witches in *Vinegar Tom*; the intrasexual inequalities in *Top Girls*; the divorce between the personal and the political in *This is a Chair*; planetary destruction in *Far Away* and *Escaped Alone*. In all of these the world does not transform into a utopian somewhere. The capitalist order that Marion so voraciously adopts in *Owners*, one that exploits the agricultural labour of the women in *Fen* and that the Skriker seeks to avenge, still has not fallen. But the experience of theatre does not end with the dramatic fiction: what happens to us in the feeling-thinking process of engaging with Churchill's dystopian critiques of capitalism and advocacy of ecological, socialist and feminist values, is also part of the story. As noted above, there is no certainty that in or beyond the theatre a recognition of a dystopic reality will occasion the desire to desire differently and/or act for change. Equally, like Someone, we may feel bewildered and at a loss to know how to make the future that did not happen, happen. Or those of us on the Left might feel incapacitated by 'the emotional experience of political defeat'. Notwithstanding the fragility of a to-be-hoped-for, healing future, the difficulty of knowing how to make it happen, or feeling the negative emotions of 'political defeat', ultimately, the 'what-if-if-only' possibility of transformation rests with us. As the ghosting of *Cloud Nine* from 1979 (the year that marked the advent of neoliberalism) into this final section emblematically evinces, that possibility depends on a *collective* desire to desire differently *and* the struggles of all those negatively impacted by a political order to transform a 'utopian nowhere place' into a real somewhere.

'In drama there is a hope of reaching people of every kind, developing a common culture and an awareness which will determine how we act – this, if anything, should be worth committing oneself to' (Churchill 1960: 451). This was Churchill's testimony to the potential power and influence of theatre at the start of her career.[59] As this Element reflects, she has committed herself to a decades-long career in theatre as a communal, artistic medium in which she sensed a capacity to engender an 'awareness' that can impact 'how we act'. Over the course of her professional lifetime, feminism and socialism have suffered many setbacks. Equally, ecological struggles have been repeatedly undermined by a failure to transform an ecologically exploitative, global capitalism. Nonetheless, Churchill has persistently urged our disidentification with capitalism and identification with the reparative triangulation of an eco-socialist feminism. As spectators of her innovative, formally shapeshifting theatre, to feel wounded by an 'awareness' of a dystopic reality into an 'anti-adaptive', resistant mode of desiring differently is to remain open to the possibility of a hopeful future, socially and ecologically.

When *What If If Only* ends, it closes with the Child Future who is 'one of the hopefuls' (Churchill 2021: 14). To the Child Future Churchill assigns the last line of the play: 'I'm going to happen' (Churchill 2021: 15). But this is only one of many possible futures. Thus, the critical, political question lingers: what will we still yet choose – 'Feminism or Death'?

---

[59] Making this observation, Churchill was comparing drama to television that at the time of writing was poised to influence 'the frame of mind of the country'. Reflecting on the 'social function' of theatre, she speculated that 'if good enough plays are written the live theatre could begin to be an important influence too' (1960: 451).

References

Adiseshiah, S. (2023). *Utopian Drama: In Search of a Genre*. London: Methuen Drama.

Aristotle (1965). *Aristotle Horace Longinus*. Trans. T. S. Dorsch. Harmondsworth: Penguin.

Aston, E. (2025). 'Dramatic Representations of "Them" and "Us" Class Struggle in Neoliberal Britain'. In B. Clarke, ed., *The Routledge Companion to Working-Class Literature*. London: Routledge, pp.283–295.

(2020). *Restaging Feminisms*. London: Palgrave Macmillan.

(2016). 'Room for Realism?' In S. Adiseshiah & L. Lepage, eds., *Twenty-First Century Drama: What Happens Now*. London: Palgrave Macmillan, pp.17–35.

(2015). 'The Skriker Royal Exchange Manchester'. Blog Post, Drama Queens Review. The Skriker: Royal Exchange Manchester | Drama Queens Review. (accessed 11 April 2024).

(2013). 'But Not That: Caryl Churchill's Political Shape Shifting at the Turn of the Millennium'. *Modern Drama*, vol. 56 (2), 145–164.

(2010). *Caryl Churchill*. 3rd ed. Tavistock: Northcote House.

(2009). 'On Collaboration: "Not Ordinary, Not Safe"'. In E. Aston & E. Diamond, eds., *The Cambridge Companion to Caryl Churchill*. Cambridge: Cambridge University Press, pp.144–162.

(2003). *Feminist Views on the English Stage: Women Playwrights 1990–2000*. Cambridge: Cambridge University Press.

Bassett, L. (2009). 'Bypassing the Logical – Performing Churchill's *Far Away*'. In J. Machon, ed., *(Syn)aesthetics: Redefining Visceral Performance*. Basingstoke: Palgrave Macmillan, pp.144–152.

BBC (1988). *The Caryl Churchill Omnibus*.

Betsko, K. & Koenig, R. eds. (1987). *Interviews with Contemporary Women Playwrights*. New York: Beech Tree.

Billington, M. (2000). Rev. of *Far Away*. *Guardian*, 1 December. Reprinted in *Theatre Record*, vol. 20, 1578.

Brook, P. (1972 [1968]). *The Empty Space*. Harmondsworth: Pelican.

Burton-Cartledge, P. (2021). *Falling Down: The Conservative Party and the Decline of Tory Britain*. London: Verso.

Campbell, B. (1987). *The Iron Ladies: Why Do Women Vote Tory?* London: Virago.

Chamberlain, M. (1977). *Fenwomen: A Portrait of Women in an English Village*. London: Virago.

Churchill C. (2021). *What If If Only*. E-book edition. London: Nick Hern.

——— (2016). *Escaped Alone*. London: Nick Hern.

——— (2008). *Plays: 4* (*Hotel, This Is a Chair, Blue Heart, Far Away, A Number, A Dream Play, Drunk Enough to Say I Love You?*). London: Nick Hern.

——— (1994). *The Skriker*. London: Nick Hern.

——— (1990a). *Plays: Two* (*Softcops, Top Girls, Fen, Serious Money*). London: Methuen.

——— (1990b). *Churchill: Shorts*. (*Lovesick, Abortive, Not Not Not Not Not Enough Oxygen, Schreber's Nervous Illness, The Hospital at the Time of the Revolution, The Judge's Wife, The After-Dinner Joke, Seagulls, Three More Sleepless Nights, Hot Fudge*). London: Nick Hern.

——— (1985). *Plays: One* (*Owners, Traps, Vinegar Tom, Light Shining in Buckinghamshire, Cloud Nine*). London: Methuen.

——— (1960). 'Not Ordinary, Not Safe: A Direction For Drama?' *The Twentieth Century*, vol. 168, November, 443–451.

Clapp, S. (2016). Rev. of *Escaped Alone*. *Observer*, 31 January. Reprinted in *Theatre Record*, vol. 36, 63.

Daly, M. (1978). *Gyn/ecology: The Metaethics of Radical Feminism*. Boston: Beacon Press.

Diamond, E. (1997). *Unmaking Mimesis*. London: Routledge.

Dolan, J. (1988). *The Feminist Spectator as Critic*. Ann Arbor: University of Michigan Press.

D'Eaubonne, F. (2022 [1974]). *Feminism or Death*. Trans. by R. Hottell. London: Verso.

Ehrenreich, B. & D. English (1973). *Witches, Midwives, and Nurses: A History of Women Healers*. New York: The Feminist Press.

Figes, E. (1978 [1970]). *Patriarchal Attitudes*. London: Virago.

Ford, B. Q., M. Feinberg, B. Lassetter, S. Thai, & A. Gatchpazian. (2023). 'The Political Is Personal: The Costs of Daily Politics'. *Journal of Personality and Social Psychology: Attitudes and Social Cognition*, 1–28.

Fraser, N. (2013). *Fortunes of Feminism: From State-Managed Capitalism to Neoliberal Crisis*. London: Verso

Fraser, N. & R. Jaeggi. (2023). *Capitalism: A Conversation in Critical Theory*. London: Verso.

Friedan, B. (2010 [1963]). *The Feminine Mystique*. London: Penguin.

Gobert, D. R. (2014). *The Theatre of Caryl Churchill*. London: Bloomsbury.

Gooch, S. (1973). 'Caryl Churchill, Author of This Month's Playtext, Talks to P & P'. *Plays and Players*, January, 40 & i of play text inset.

Griffin, S. (1978). *Woman and Nature: The Roaring Inside Her*. New York: Harper & Row.

Hall, S. (2011). 'The Neo-Liberal Revolution'. *Cultural Studies*, vol. 25 (6), 705–728.

(1988). *The Hard Road to Renewal: Thatcherism and the Crisis of the Left*. London: Verso.

Hanna, G., ed. (1991). *Monstrous Regiment: A Collective Celebration*. London: Nick Hern.

(1989). 'Writing Our Own History, Feminist Theatricals'. *Trouble and Strife*, 16, Summer, 47–52.

Kellaway, K. (2015). '*Light Shining in Buckingamshire* Review'. *Guardian*, 26 April. Light Shining in Buckinghamshire review– arguments fought with fire | Caryl Churchill | The Guardian (accessed 8 March 2024).

Little, R. & McLaughlin E. (2007). *The Royal Court Theatre Inside Out*. London: Oberon.

Macaulay, A. (2000). Rev. *Far Away*. *Financial Times*, 4 December. Reprinted in *Theatre Record*, vol. 20, 1577.

Marks, E. & I. de Courtivron, eds. (1981). *New French Feminisms*. Brighton: The Harvester Press.

McFerran, A. (1977). 'The Theatre's (Somewhat) Angry Young Women'. *Time Out*, 21–27, October, 13–15.

McRobbie, A. (2000). *Feminism and Youth Culture*. 2nd ed. London: Macmillan.

Mitchell, J. (2021). 'Raymond Williams: Tomorrow Is Also Yesterday's Day'. *European Journal of Cultural Studies*, vol. 24 (4), 1035–1043.

(1971). *Woman's Estate*. Harmondsworth: Penguin.

Monbiot, G. (1997). 'Turning the World Upside Down'. Theatre Programme, *Light Shining in Buckinghamshire*, Royal National Theatre, n.p.

Monstrous Regiment (1982). 'Production Note'. In M. Wandor, ed., *Plays by Women: Volume One*. London: Methuen, pp.40–42.

Home – Monstrous Regiment (website; accessed 8 March 2024).

Morton, T. (2010). *The Ecological Thought*. Cambridge, MA: Harvard University Press.

Mouffe, C. (2013). *Agonistics: Thinking the World Politically*. London: Verso.

(2005). *On the Political*. London: Routledge.

Murray, A. (2019). *The Fall and Rise of the British Left*. London: Verso.

Plumwood, V. (1993). *Feminism and the Mastery of Nature*. London: Routledge.

Proctor, H. (2024). *Burnout: The Emotional Experience of Political Defeat*. London Verso.

Reinelt, J. (1994). *After Brecht: British Epic Theater*. Ann Arbor: University of Michigan Press.

Roberts, P. (2008). *About Churchill: The Playwright & the Work*. London: Faber & Faber.

Royal National Theatre (1994). Theatre Programme, *The Skriker*.

Thatcher, M. (1982). 'Women in a Changing World'. Margaret Thatcher Foundation. Speech on Women in a changing World (1st Dame Margery Corbett-Ashby Memorial Lecture) (accessed 11 April 2024).

Thompson, J. (2019). 'Top Girls at the National Theatre', *Evening Standard*, 1 April. Top Girls at the National Theatre: How Caryl Churchill's land mark play feels today, according to cast past and present | London Evening Standard | Evening Standard (accessed 31 March 2024).

Toynbee, P. & D. Walker. (2015). *Cameron's Coup: How the Tories Took Britain to the Brink*. London: Faber & Faber.

Trueman, M. (2016). 'James Macdonald on Caryl Churchill's *Escaped Alone: 'I'm Drawn to Plays I Don't Know How to Do'*. *Independent*, 18 January. James Macdonald on Caryl Churchill's 'Escaped Alone': 'I'm drawn to plays Idon't know how to do' | The Independent | The Independent (accessed 20 June 2024).

Vettese, T. & D. Pendergrass (2022). *Half-Earth Socialism: A Plan to Save the Future from Extinction, Climate Change, and Pandemics*. London: Verso.

Walter, N. (1999). *The New Feminism*. London: Virago.

Wiegand, C. (2016). 'Sunshine and Terrible Rage: Linda Bassett on Caryl Churchill's *Escaped Alone*. *Guardian*, 10 February. Sunshine and terrible rage: Linda Bassett on Caryl Churchill's Escaped Alone | Theatre | The Guardian (accessed 20 June, 2024).

Williams, R. (1983). *Towards 2000*. Harmondsworth: Penguin.

(1977). *Marxism and Literature*. Oxford: Oxford University Press.

(1965 [1961]). *The Long Revolution*. Harmondsworth: Pelican.

Acknowledgements

For their unerring, supportive company, my heartfelt thanks go to Daniel and Merryn, Maggie and Tim, and the joyous little ones – William, Leo, Noah, Eden and newest arrival, Elijah. I am indebted to those who joined the conversations around the philosophers' table at Theritas, Acharavai, Corfu, where this Element was conceived: Dimitris, Ellie, Jelena, Olga, and Antonios, whose capacity for philosophising into the early hours is unparalleled. Finally, thanks to Melissa Sihra and Emily Hockley for their kind assistance in the commissioning of this project.

Women Theatre Makers

Elaine Aston
Lancaster University

Elaine Aston is internationally acclaimed for her feminism and theatre research. Her monographs include *Caryl Churchill* (1997); *Feminism and Theatre* (1995); *Feminist Theatre Practice* (1999); *Feminist Views on the English Stage* (2003); and *Restaging Feminisms* (2020). She has served as Senior Editor of Theatre Research International (2010–12) and President of the International Federation for Theatre Research (2019–23).

Melissa Sihra
Trinity College Dublin

Melissa Sihra is Associate Professor in Drama and Theatre Studies at Trinity College Dublin. She is author of *Marina Carr: Pastures of the Unknown* (2018) and editor of *Women in Irish Drama: A Century of Authorship and Representation* (2007). She was President of the Irish Society for Theatre Research (2011–15) and is currently researching a feminist historiography of the Irish playwright and co-founder of the Abbey Theatre, Lady Augusta Gregory.

Advisory Board

Nobuko Anan, *Kansai University, Japan*
Awo Mana Asiedu, *University of Ghana*
Ana Bernstein, *UNIRIO, Brazil*
Elin Diamond, *Rutgers, USA*
Bishnupriya Dutt, *JNU, India*
Penny Farfan, *University of Calgary, Canada*
Lesley Ferris, *Ohio State University, USA*
Lisa FitzPatrick, *University of Ulster, Northern Ireland*
Lynette Goddard, *Royal Holloway, University of London, UK*
Sarah Gorman, *Roehampton University, UK*
Aoife Monks, *Queen Mary, London University, UK*
Kim Solga, *Western University, Canada*
Denise Varney, *University of Melbourne, Australia*

About the Series

This innovative, inclusive series showcases women-identifying theatre makers from around the world. Expansive in chronological and geographical scope, the series encompasses practitioners from the late nineteenth century onwards and addresses a global, comprehensive range of creatives – from playwrights and performers to directors and designers.

Cambridge Elements

Women Theatre Makers

Elements in the Series

Maya Rao and Indian Feminist Theatre
Bishnupriya Dutt

Xin Fengxia and the Transformation of China's Ping Opera
Siyuan Liu

Emma Rice's Feminist Acts of Love
Lisa Peck

Women Making Shakespeare in the Twenty-First Century
Kim Solga

Clean Break Theatre Company
Caoimhe McAvinchey, Sarah Bartley, Deborah Dean and Anne-marie Greene

#WakingTheFeminists and the Data-Driven Revolution in Irish Theatre
Claire Keogh

The Theatre of Louise Lowe
Miriam Haughton

Ellen Terry, Shakespeare, and Suffrage in Australia and New Zealand
Kate Flaherty

Performing Female Intimacy in Japan's Takarazuka Revue
Nobuko Anan

Feminist Imagining in Polish and Ukrainian Theatres
Ewa Bal and Kasia Lech

Caryl Churchill's Eco-Socialist Feminism
Elaine Aston

A full series listing is available at: www.cambridge.org/EWTM

For EU product safety concerns, contact us at Calle de José Abascal, 56–1°,
28003 Madrid, Spain or eugpsr@cambridge.org.

www.ingramcontent.com/pod-product-compliance
Lightning Source LLC
LaVergne TN
LVHW011857060526
838200LV00054B/4379